MW01059156

RAW

Endorsements for RAW

"As a student Rebecca was thoughtful and discerning, and as a writer she continues to engage. *RAW Inner Workings of a Reawakened Soul* is an honest and sincere glimpse into the journey for life's meaning and purpose with the God of the universe who beckons us to call him...*Father*. Rebecca's disarming style, concise insights, and practical applications make this book a helpful and powerful read for anyone searching for significance in life."

Jeff Martell, *Lead Campus Pastor Grace Church, Barberton Campus*

"Each of us is on a spiritual journey trying to figure out what we believe and why we believe these things. Rebecca gives us an honest, genuine and raw look into her spiritual journey with a conversational and relational style. The book has the power to connect to many of us who are working out their faith and looking for real life answers to difficult questions."

Cody Clark, *Senior Pastor Cross Point Christian Church*

"*RAW Inner Workings of a Reawakened Soul* is a fresh look at what God truly wants each of us to be. Rebecca reminds us that we are all created in His image, yet we are all fully unique in that creation. It's OK if you don't fit the 'perfect Christian mold'. God is going to use you in your brokenness and in your rawness, in His perfect way."

Jenny Kuhns, *Lover of Jesus*

RAW

Inner Workings of a Reawakened Soul

Rebecca Greenfield

RAW

Copyright © 2017 by Rebecca Greenfield

All rights reserved. No part of this book may be reproduced or utilized in any form or by any means, electronic or mechanical, including photocopying, recording, or by any information storage and retrieval system, without permission in writing from the publisher.

Library of Congress Cataloging-in-Publication Data

Library of Congress Control Number: 2017918299

Greenfield, Rebecca

    RAW : inner workings of a reawakened soul / Rebecca Greenfield
          p. cm.

    ISBN 978-0-692-98800-8 (paperback, printed)

All Scripture quotations, unless otherwise indicated, are taken from the Holy Bible, New International Version®, NIV®. Copyright © 1973, 1978, 1984, 2011 by Biblica, Inc.™ Used by permission. All rights reserved.

Cover & Interior design: Jennie Gold

Cover Photography: Alessio Lin

Printed in the United States of America

To the ones who have loved me more than life

My parents, Bill and Dixie

To the ones who have always been there for me

My grandparents and Uncle, Jean, Lester and Rex

To the ones who adopted me as their own

Ron and Morie

To the ones who have counseled me during late nights and long conversations

My dearest friends

To the love of my life and the one who has never left my side

My husband, Chris

To the author and redeemer of my life

My savior, Jesus

Words will never fully describe the immeasurable love and gratitude I have for each of you. May you always know the irreplaceable role you play in my life.

Table of Contents

Author's Note

It's scary to put yourself out there—out there on the line, exposed, open and available for all to see. You risk a lot. You risk being thought a fool. You risk being too vulnerable. You risk being criticized, judged, and laughed at. When I first began this book, I was excited and ready to share. I've dreamed about writing a book for years and hoped that one day I'd be able to help others through the same medium God has used countless times to help me. I'm still excited to write, to express, and to create, but now the weight of the risk has set in. I've begun to wonder what people will think. What will they like? What will they hate? Will they see me as stronger, or weaker? Will they judge me as smarter, or dumber? Will I be thought of as too conservative? Too liberal? Too annoying? The questions thrash against my spirit.

I assume that some people will read my book not because they truly want to but because they are just curious. Some may know me as an everyday person, living an everyday life, offering nothing special or unique. There will be some who don't know my flaws— inside and out—like those who coexist alongside me. I suppose that to them everything I say will be much easier to digest. At least maybe (cross my fingers) they'll have fewer criticisms because they can't compare my everyday life to my inner thoughts. I think about my coworkers and my church—how they will critique my book—if they even read it. The stranger down the road who may pick up a copy and rip it to shreds won't come as close to crushing my self-esteem or dashing my dreams as those close to me. And yet I wouldn't expect anything except honesty from the reader. A person writes to be heard, not necessarily to be liked. Just as I read a book and make my many critical assessments of that work, I would only anticipate the same treatment from my readers.

It's weird, but when you write, or maybe anytime you create something, you want there to be a purpose. You want there to be an answer to something. Whether it's an answer to the callings and yearnings of others or a tool used by God to bring finality to a question—you want it to have a point. While having dinner one evening with a close friend, I told her I was writing a book. I always hesitate to tell others that I'm writing a book because it makes me feel uneasy. I immediately think I can hear their internal dialogue, something to the effect of, "Yeah, right, like anything will ever come of that. People always say they are going to do something, and it never happens." I figure people will think of it as an old quilt that was started and was always meant to be finished but remains tattered and half-sewn in the basement. Or they will compare it to a project like cleaning the attic—something they've been talking about doing for twelve years now but decide that it would be better to wait and finish next winter instead. After I told my friend the news, she handled it with such genuine grace and encouragement that her words rested on my insecurity like a full meal on an empty stomach. I'm still grateful. I remember her asking me, "Do you ever feel the pressure or the need to come up with an answer or a point when sometimes there really isn't one?" She'd tapped into something significant to the core of not only me but of us as human beings. We're pragmatic. We want there to be a reason behind the experience and a purpose for all the work. I've found it tiresome to always be looking for a solution, a valid point, a helpful answer. The burden weighs heavily on me each time I reach into my creative self, but yet I still carry it. There is this strange tendency, as I write, to want to develop something unsaid —to grant a revelation that echoes deep into the psyche. I strain for my work to yield inspiration, vitality... significance. And sadly, the idea of middling work that receives only adequate, less than raving praise bruises my ego a bit. If that's the case, I presume, then, that I've lost the point myself. The purpose of creating is not to receive applause but rather to enjoy the gift of acting out one's God-bearing image.

I think it's okay not to have the answer and maybe even to not have a point. I guess it's okay to live in the hesitations between breaths. Maybe that's a little bit closer to how life really is. We want everything to come to a conclusion, wrapped up like a package, tied and complete. But many times in life we don't have the answer. We go around with unresolved questions, that may never settle. Real life doesn't bring closure. Most of the time is spent learning, not concluding.

I think what might not be okay, though, is listening to all the "what if" voices. I can't please everyone even if I want to so badly. But there are fires God starts in us that nearly burn out, that smolder and die. I think, though, that He keeps trying to light it even when it's completely soaked with water—even when there's only one small log left. Over and over again, He attempts to light it. And I think we often ignore it and even blow it out again ourselves. Our fears consume our fire, and we're left inhaling the smoke. And that chokes out our spirit. Shot down, shut down.

Sergei Rachmaninoff has written some of the most brilliant and masterful classical music ever performed. Its wonder and technique is vast in its challenge and unrivaled in its beauty. I once read an article about him that explained the history behind his Concerto No. 2 in C Minor, Op. 18 masterpiece. When Rachmaninoff attended the premiere of his work, *First Symphony* in March 1897, he arrived at the concert hall only to find the conductor drunk and the performance a near-wreck. Cesar Cui, a prominent critic at that time, said,

> If there were a conservatory in Hell, and if one of its talented students were to compose a programme symphony based on the story of the Ten Plagues of Egypt, and if he were to compose a symphony like Mr. Rachmaninov's, then he would have fulfilled his task brilliantly and would delight Hell's inhabitants.[1]

The whole event caused Rachmaninoff to enter into a deep depression that lasted more than three years. The depression was so severe that he nearly ended all efforts to continue any further compositions. Finally, his family got involved and forced him to see a psychiatrist who was known to cure depression through hypnosis. The doctor made Rachmaninoff repeat over and over again in his hypnotic trance, "You will begin to write a concerto...you will work with great facility...the concerto will be of excellent quality."[2] After three months, Rachmaninoff began to wake up to the inspiration that had lain dormant in him for so many years, and he began to create his magnum opus, Concert No. 2 in C Minor, Op. 18. As I read this article by the dimly lit stage and house lights prior to hearing the orchestra execute its magnificence, I was naturally surprised. An accomplished, talented man whose compositions have been performed countless times for over a century had almost been shot down. Such splendor would forever have been withheld from millions of ears and—even worse—such purpose would have forever stayed trapped within a man destined to create.

What I create may remain unrecognized, unnoticed, or read and discarded by countless many. My worst fears and the taunting judgments may come to fruition. My spirit could become crushed in ways I didn't expect. But what matters is knowing who I am, and that is something that cannot be taken from me. God can use my writings to reach people in ways I did not even anticipate because God is bigger than my insecurities and shortcomings. I need not compromise for the sake of rendering an answer. The pressures we put on ourselves for the need to fit in, the need to be accepted, and the need to preserve our fragile egos have been afforded far too much sway over the image of God we carry inside of us. I wish I could turn off the risk like a light switch, along with all the presumed unspoken commentary that I suspect is being thought of by both those who love and hate my work. If only it were that simple. I would have powered out a long time ago. Regardless of what others may think of me or my work, the most important thing is who I am to God. And if I live out what He lays upon my heart, resulting in even just one tiny seed of truth being planted in a passerby, then my work is done. I can't please the world, but I can live out the fire, or even just the dimly lit spark beneath the smoky haze of my creative nature. Even if the rest of the world doesn't like it, at least I'll have received the internal reward of living it out.

Chapter 1

Relatability

It's fall, and the leaves are changing. Ah, the smells and sounds of autumn...golden, burnt hues that kiss an auburn aura and press against the dark, heavy clouds of fall. To be honest, I think I'm one of the few who are not all that fond of fall. To me, the season is reminiscent of school buses, shorter days, and the daunting realization that snow and flu season are right around the corner. I guess that's the pessimist in me: I always find myself dealing with a somewhat chronic case of melancholy and sentimentalism during this season. However, I must confess that a little piece of me enjoys autumn a small smidgen simply for its undeniable beauty. This season is like a blend of sour and sweet, like entering a cool swimming pool during a warm day. That initial "hold-my-breath" shock stunts my appreciation for the refreshing splendor of thirty gallons of water.

I find myself wandering through fall, reminiscing about previous seasons, and feeling very introspective and comparative by nature. These past few weeks, during another beautiful fall season in Ohio, I have been searching for what it is that I'm feeling the desire, or the need, to do. I'm a very emotional person, which is mostly a plus but too often a negative attribute. My brain never shuts off, and my heart keeps working on overtime. I'm stuck in my search, left with snippets here and there of what the internal me is saying. After each soul search, I come up for air only to find myself drawn continually to art. But that is such a broad topic. Art can be anything—music, pictures, sculptures—some even say graffiti. I'm intrigued by art. I never used to consider myself an artistic person because I couldn't draw a picture if my life depended on it. My

"Picasso masterpieces" consist of kindergarten stick figures of Dad, Mom, and Fluffy the cat.

However, what I've found, and am deeply convinced about, is that writing is an art. I can't draw, I can't paint, I can sing but I hate performing. So I claim writing as my art. Words are beautiful to me. They enable me to express my deepest emotions—carrying with them underlying emphasis, nuance, and unique power. They have the ability to make us laugh, make us cry, make us mad, make us love, and make us come alive inside. Words are so much more than a compilation of letters. The formation of poetry or lyrical compositions tag-team with another form of art: music. And the two, in tandem, can stir a heart so deeply that one's soul threatens to burst.

I sat here tonight reading. I love reading. That was a surprising love affair. I'm the girl who claimed *Charlotte's Web* as her favorite book until high school and whose mother read the high school honors English summer reading books to her so she could actually complete them before the first day of school. Yeah, that's me. What a champ! I hated reading, until I read the last hundred pages of *The Count of Monte Cristo* during my senior year of high school. (The first half was accomplished by CliffsNotes and the excellent film starring Jim Caviezel.) Soon after college hit, I found the wonderful genre of Christian books. Finally, books started to connect with my soul just a tad bit more than Wilbur the "radiant pig." Nevertheless, Wilbur, you will always hold a special place in my heart.

The various authors' compositions sandwiched between my

fingertips have acted as house-call counselors, physicians, preachers, and friends as they taught me about life, God, and the truth that permeates. Solace and peace emancipated from the thick, black ink, rolled up and out to become absorbed by my heart to quiet the inner cry. The Holy Spirit is far from limited in how He moves, and with each book I've feverishly read, He has continued to plant and water a garden of truth and promise in my life.

As much as I love the art of the vernacular, I don't claim to be a lingual genius. I didn't make it in the spelling bee, and I'll never understand why you can't end a sentence with a preposition. I'm a big fan of inventing new words—well, not really intentionally, but for the sake of my pride, I'd like to claim it's not my stupidity but rather my intention to create words that don't exist. I once created the word *pathetible*. Its meaning connotes a clever combination of the words *pathetic* and *pitiful*. When I was little, I was scared of the water. I didn't know how to swim, I didn't like getting water in my ears or up my nose, and so I had a lovely pink Barbie life jacket that kept me safe in water that was three feet deep. (Sadly, you don't realize what a true nerd you are until you take time to recount all the specific details). My dad decided to give me what he called "swimming lessons." In my panic and frustration at being forced to learn how to swim, I told him that the whole thing was pathetible. And so the word has been carried on for years.

I'm also notorious for using a correct phrase or word in an inappropriate manner. Recently, I told someone I was going to "recant" their gift. Well, that word, I discovered, is not synonymous with "take back." You only "recant" words or beliefs, not physical items like a flannel shirt. Or what about the phrase, "Rob Peter to pay Paul"? Somehow I managed to say something about robbing from Peter to steal from Paul to give to Mary. I don't know why, but I always want to include Peter, Paul, and Mary, the 1960s performers of "Puff, the Magic Dragon." Too many names! And this is why I'm always hesitant to venture outside my small circle of vocabulary words. *Stick with what you know.* Sometimes I feel like Moses: Speaking isn't my forte. Verbalizing my thoughts is less efficient than penning them. Ah, the beauty of writing—it lets you think before you speak. Plus, there is always the added bonus of automatic spell-check and Merriam-Webster's online dictionary.

On that note, I would like to intentionally create a new word. It's a word that has been floating around inside my head for months—maybe years—but I can never use it in conversation because, well, I just can't bear the dumbfounded looks. The word is *relatableness.* It means "the ability or experience of relating." It isn't found in Webster's or on Dictionary.com. For our purposes, I'm defining *relatability*, or *relatableness,* in a possessive nature. It expresses the idea that an object, person, or experience has the ability to relate to you. And by relating to you, it connects you more deeply to divine insight from God. It's a ministry of relating in which God uses a certain event, song, or movie (basically anything He chooses) to reveal more of Himself to you. It's the resonance of truth.

I discovered the gift of relatableness when I was going through a time of searching. If you've ever been in a place where the

Christian bubble has popped, the real world has become confusing, and this so-called "loving God" has become as distant and perplexing as an angry genie, you suddenly appreciate input from outside the Christian circle. It has a refreshing and intriguing effect on the heart and mind. But the input tends to hit a little closer to home (and to truth) than the Christian clichés that seem to spew from happy people's mouths when you're in a time of wrenching emotion. If you've been there, you know exactly what I mean. Why is it that happy people are suddenly so annoying when life sucks?

During that time, it didn't feel as though God was near... but neither did it feel as though He'd left me. He seemed not to be talking at all, and if He was talking, it was in another language. But what I came to discover was that He *was* talking—He just wasn't yelling. And when He was whispering, He was doing it in a foreign, but still recognizable, language. It was a language that was refreshing, unprecedented, and gracious. I heard Him speak in a way that was unfamiliar to me. This way was through relatability. It wasn't an audible voice, like a man on a microphone telling me what to do, who to be, and where to go. It was through circumstances, through events, and, commonly, through things (e.g., quotes, people, lyrics, movies) that didn't fit within the Christian bubble. And I loved it. It was clear, it was merciful, it was beautiful...it was raw!

Sometimes, I remember, God would impress things on my heart that came completely out of left field. I was once listening to a Dave Matthew song on my drive home, and suddenly God just seemed to unveil the clearest understanding and picture of the state of my heart. And no, it wasn't condemning—"thou shalt not listen to such depraved music." It was a seed of truth, a moment of clarity, and a feeling of comfort. I also remember watching movies that seemed to completely describe what I was going through in my life. And just by the sheer ability to relate to my situation, it was as if God were ministering to me powerfully, sometimes ministering to my heart more deeply than the previous Sunday's sermon. I began to realize that many times, maybe more often than we even acknowledge, God speaks through "un-Christian," secular things to minister to our hearts. God doesn't use only the Church or its doctrine, ideas, and events to speak to our hearts.

By no means am I rejecting God's use of the Church (e.g., sermons, Christians, and worship music) to connect with our souls. I remember reading books by Christian authors and underlining nearly every sentence because something they said resonated so deeply with my soul. My books were heavily laden with stars, scribbles, and lines that looked as though a drunk had read them, but I couldn't help myself. They were singing my song, they were speaking my language, and they said something that related totally to where I was and what I was going through. I'd listen to podcasts and practically wore out CDs after playing them over and over again in my car. Each book, each sermon, and each song planted a seed of truth and revealed more of God's heart.

My point is that God is a god who is not limited by temporal categories of good or bad, Christian or secular, blessing or curse to speak to the hearts of humans. He can use anything and everything, if we're willing to listen and able to discern. There is a quote used in the movie *Eat Pray Love*,[3] in which the actress Julia Roberts, playing the true-life author, Liz Gilbert, states,

> In the end, I've come to believe in something I call "The Physics of the Quest." A force in nature governed by laws as real as the laws of gravity. The rule of Quest Physics goes something like this: If you're brave enough to leave behind everything familiar and comforting, which can be anything from your house to bitter, old resentments, and set out on a truth-seeking journey, either externally or internally, and if you are truly willing to regard everything that happens to you on that journey as a clue and if you accept everyone you meet along the way as a teacher and if you are prepared, most of all, to face and forgive some very difficult realities about yourself, then the truth will not be withheld from you.

And this, my friends, is the power of relatability. Christian or atheist, we're all on a journey. We're learning about ourselves, about God, about who we are to God, and about loss, sorrow, hope, and the unpredictable circumstances that sneak up on us. Ultimately, we're all searching for truth. There is a thirst for it, and whether or not you believe in Jesus, He was absolutely right when He described that each of us has a thirst and a hunger for truth. Some choose to ignore it, and some choose to allow it to propel them on a quest.

Everyone handles this quest differently. I would consider myself a pretty open person. You ask me a personal question, and I will usually share my heart with you (unless of course, you are some creeper who doesn't understand the proper social cues as to what or what not to say to a young female). I love meeting other people who I can connect with on a soul-to-soul level, even if they aren't believers in the same God, or in a god at all. What these people offer is real and relatable. They offer themselves, the raw, broken, true parts of their inner selves, and that I find fascinating. I love getting into conversations with agnostics or atheists. I bond with those who confess that life has really gotten them down and that they aren't really sure which end is up. I connect with seekers who are wondering if there is a god, and if so, does that god even know their name. I respect those who, on the quest for truth, admit that most of the time they swear that they feel as though they're paddling upstream. Whether their story be joyous or tragic, I'm honored when someone feels sufficiently comfortable with me to express their heart.

I value honesty and openness, and when I write, I project those values into my stories. I want to tell you my journey. I want to share my heart, raw with emotion, torn with shame, glazed with hope, or grounded with peace. However, I recognize that in the same manner I respect openness, another person respects privacy. Ask them to describe their most embarrassing moment, and they will tell you about the time they snorted while laughing (never once hinting at the time they left the bathroom with toilet paper stuck to their shoe or the evening they spilled marinara sauce down the front of their blouse on their first—and *last*—date with the guy from work). They respect their personal boundaries. What they will share will be minimal, and the rest of the information is frankly "not your business." As with everything, there are opposing views on what and how much to share about one's life. And truthfully, both views should be respected, in moderation. Truly, not everyone needs nor wants to know that coleslaw gives you gas, neither does it hurt to confess that the tear you shed was actually real.

There is a wedding tradition from ancient Jewish culture, in which the bride and groom get married under a canopy called a *chuppah*₄—a covering that represents a Jewish home and is open on all four sides, like Abraham's house, to represent hospitality. The chuppah was also symbolic of God's blessing, protection, and recognition of the covenant between the husband and wife. It was a reminder that the bride and groom were creating their own house, their own space, their own privacy, and their own life with one another. A relationship open to their community, but still personal to them and ordained in the presence of God. Marriage is one of the most powerful representations of Christ's love for the Church. There are many different analogies God uses to describe His relationship with us—a shepherd and his sheep (John 10), a master and his slave (Romans 6:22), a father and his child (Hebrews 12:5-6), a king and his heir (Romans 8:17)—but of all these analogies, the most powerful to me is that of a groom and his bride.

I am always so excited to share, "Do you know what God is doing in my life? I think God might be leading me...yesterday, I was questioning God about..." and on and on. Like I said, I'm an open book. However, this idea of chuppah applies to me and God, my groom. There are matters of my heart that should always remain exactly that... matters of my heart. Yes, faith is to be lived out in community. That is essential...healthy, and we're even called to do so (Hebrews 10:25). However, there is a chuppah of the heart, a place of intimacy shared between you and the Creator. A place where thoughts are exposed, honesty is revealed, acceptance is found, searching is answered unanswered, and hope is budding. Not all things are meant to be shared. Not even all *good* things are meant to be shared. Some things are meant to be pondered, relished and reserved. Ecclesiastes so adequately expresses certain fundamental facts of life, "There is a time for everything, and a season for every activity under heaven...a time to be silent and a time to speak" (Ecc 3:1 and 7b). Yes, sometimes we need to hear wise input from others. Some decisions need to be talked about before being made. But some whispers from God are meant to be treasured in our hearts, because if they are blurted out prematurely, they lose the value and power that would have been gained if we would have allowed them to marinate within our soul.

I remember reading in the Gospels how the angel told Mary something or how Mary was observing certain events concerning Jesus' birth; for example, "But Mary treasured up all these things and pondered them in her heart." (Luke 2:19). Every time I would read that, it stuck with me. Mary didn't find the need to discuss it, shout it, or "run it past" a few people to get their opinions on it. She took the gift God gave her and pondered and treasured it. There, in her heart of hearts, it was protected; there it was useful, there it was effective—not exposed to others—but held captive in the chamber of her soul.

Our faith should be lived in community and should be openly discussed; praise God we have the right and the freedom to do that here in the United States. Talk about your faith with others, tell others what God is doing in your life, chew over the hard questions... ask for input. In those moments, the Divine is as present and real as the next breath you breathe. But treasure solitude with your Creator. Don't forget the chuppah of your heart. Wait to share what is budding within. Hold back if only a part is revealed. Carry the whisper in the depth of your soul. In its time and place, let it emerge in full bloom. Hold sacred both the privacy and openness of your soul.

During my years of searching, I found that you must be honest with yourself and be open to truth in whatever form it comes. Whether you find truth inside the Church or outside the Christian bubble, truth is truth. And all truth is of God. Relatableness is when God uses this truth, which is packaged in all forms, to shine His light on your pain, your convictions, your regrets, your questions, your misperceptions, your hope, your misbehaviors, and your unfulfilled dreams to bring clarity. During my searching, I've found that He speaks one seed of truth at a time. Soon those seeds mature and develop into transformation. Before transformation seems even remotely possible, these seeds seem scattered, stunted, and disordered. But keep charging forward on the quest. Protect the chuppah of your heart. God will meet you on the journey if you let Him. You will find relatability if your eyes are open, your ears are hearing, and your heart is malleable.

My hope with this book is to be relatable. I did not set out to illustrate "the five steps of becoming a good Christian," to tell you that your beliefs are right or wrong, or to outline the heritage of doctrinal facticity. And although those things hold their necessary place in the history and tradition of the Church of Jesus Christ, my goal is to deal more with the heart and less with the scholastics. I do not expect you to agree with all I say, and I am in no way attempting to claim that I'm inerrant in my thoughts or viewpoints. I pray that you will be blessed by relating to my stories, questions, and feelings. My goal is to put on paper what has been swarming in your head— to be the underline, scribbles, and stars as you read. I long to aid in your personal experience with God and hopefully be a forum for revealing more truth to you about His character. My greatest hope with this book is that you might be ministered to by the art and power of relatability.

Chapter 2

The Weight of Waiting

Sometimes the process is more important than the answer. We are a culture of the here and now. Get off the exit of any highway and observe a mecca of food on the go—Burger King, McDonald's, Wendy's, Arby's, Dairy Queen, Sonic. And if the grease makes your gallbladder spasm a little, and you happen to just not be in the mood to supersize your diet or your waist, snatch a sandwich at Subway. It's grab and go—no time and no money. We're like cars on empty— rushing our way to the next BP to fill up and driving 70 mph the whole time. Efficiency equals productivity, and productivity equals success. Moving forward is the American way, and if you are not moving forward, well, then, you are in that dreaded, failed-feeling, "avoid-at-all-costs" state of being...stuck.

I remember feeling stuck for years. It's almost its own form of suffering. You watch the rest of the world move on, happily, gracefully, and what appears to be easily, while you're stuck so bad it's as if you are caged in a Truman Show sort of phenomenon that enables the world and the laws of physics to conspire against you. Your heart begins to ache for "what could be"; you're like a mouse in a trap.

I've always said that Facebook is the place where lonely hearts go. Social media can be a killer. In the years I've felt stuck, I would log myself onto Facebook. There, I would find a plethora of happy people with happy lives, in happy photos, creating happy memories. I would click from page to page and read people's statuses: *Oh, they got engaged...of course,* and *She got a new job,* and *Isn't that just the cutest house they officially own now?* or *When did they have twins? Really*?? Then came the self-assessment...I was an adult woman living in a bright pink bedroom in my parents' house that was still adorned with a puppy-kitty border and baby pink carpeting, all carefully selected via my chic, 12-year-old interior decorating eye. I was still getting over the loss of my ex-boyfriend, which had happened two and a half years earlier, still applying for jobs in my field even though I had literally sent out 124 resumes to no avail, and still searching about whether or not my faith was secure in Christ or whether I even believed in Christ at all. I was in nine weddings during those two and half years. I was starting to feel like Katherine Heigl from *27 Dresses*. Each wedding made me think of my ex. Each wedding made me think of my stagnant life. I remember sobbing on my drive home after one of the rehearsal dinners because the bride and I were no longer as close as we once were, and her soon-to-be husband was who she was dating when I had been dating my ex. I logged on to Facebook as if it were my job. I checked my email incessantly. I was like a starving adolescent who keeps going to the fridge only to find ham loaf and Brussels sprouts, wishing there was some chocolate cake and pizza rolls. Finally, I realized that the reason I kept checking my phone, kept logging onto Facebook, and kept viewing my inbox was because I was waiting for something to finally change and desperately hoping that change was one text message or email away.

Those days were a struggle, not because of the weddings or the pink bedroom but because I was trying everything in my power to move forward but couldn't. No matter how hard I tried, I couldn't do it. My heart wouldn't move past my ex. The job market was flooded, and there was absolutely no demand in my field. My faith was being uprooted and changed, but as hard as I tried, I couldn't force God to reveal things to me faster. I felt utterly and miserably stuck. I remember trying to find health insurance, and even that wasn't successful. I got quoted a premium of over $600 and was denied a couple times. One particular New Year's Eve was the final straw. I broke down crying after finding out that I'd been denied by a health insurance company again, and I was alone on yet another New Year's Eve, still missing my ex from two years before. Happy New Year! Another kiss-less, date-less, broken night to welcome in another kiss-less, date-less, broken year! Oh, joy!

Slowly, as each spring morphed into another summer, and each summer faded into another fall, things began to change. I finally found some peace with God and recommitted my life to Christ. I got a new job, although it *still* wasn't in my field. I switched from rehanging clothes on a rack at Kohl's to administering electric stimulation therapy to chiropractic patients. Shock therapy! I received a pay raise from $7.50 to a whopping $8.50 an hour. So much for the power of a bachelor's degree! And I got health insurance that didn't make me sell my right kidney just to pay the monthly premium. Still didn't make enough to move out on my own. Still was sending resume after resume out to hospitals that weren't even hiring. Still mourning the loss of my ex. Still stuck. It was as if I had one foot super-glued to the floor and one foot forward. I wasn't walking forward; I was only a foot ahead.

It's agonizing—the waiting, the confusion, the crying out to

God but not really hearing much back. You feel lonely, as if you're in a club all of your own. You failed the 10th grade, while the rest moved on and graduated. Sometimes it can almost feel worse being stuck in limbo than moving uncomfortably into new territory. Like a bad traffic jam, you'd rather take back roads that add on miles and time than to sit for hours in a gridlocked pile-up, wondering how much longer the wait.

Although the walls feel quite confining and the air is stagnant, God doesn't waste the pause. In its time—its proper time—God brings about and fulfills longings of the heart in ways that are right, and even at some points that can seem almost miraculous. But you never appreciate the miracles, learn the lessons, or see the reasons without going through the process first. During those difficult years, I kept begging God for answers—for the ending. I wanted to know the timing, and I wanted to know the next step. "Just tell me the right step, God, and I will do it." I wanted the results without the pain, the maturing without the growth. Why wouldn't I? It's only natural for us to want to avoid heartache and pain, and it's even more natural for us to want to do everything in our power to expedite those moments so we don't have to be tent dwellers in the land of suffering.

During that season, I read the following passage, Hosea 2:7–8, 14, 16:

> Therefore I will block her path with thornbushes; I will wall her in so that she cannot find her way. She will chase after her lovers but not catch them; she will look for them but not find them. Then she will say, "I will go back to my husband as at first, for then I was

better off than now." She has not acknowledged that I was the one who gave her the grain, the new wine and oil, who lavished on her the silver and gold— which they used for Baal. Therefore I am now going to allure her; I will lead her into the wilderness and speak tenderly to her. In that day, declares the LORD, you will call me "my husband"; you will no longer call me "my master."

That's exactly how I felt. My paths were blocked, and my efforts were knocked down, not because God was mean but because He loved me enough to not allow me to escape Him and thereby miss out on an intimate, deepened relationship with Him. I realized there were longings in my heart that He would not fulfill until I learned certain lessons He was teaching me. When I understood that, I was filled with gratitude, recognized that my God was my all and everything, and felt complete fulfillment in Him...not! Let's get real. I handled it as well as a two-year-old whose mother just told her "no" to the grape lollipop she was grabbing. True, I was grateful for having some light shed on why I had to be left in the wilderness for what felt like another forty years, but I was also kicking and screaming at the realization that my time in that season was not up. There was much to learn and much time to learn it in.

Although I speak of those days as "trials" and "tough," I am aware that they didn't represent the true tests in life. In many ways, they were the American problems of an early adult in her twenties. Nonetheless, God used that time to reveal much about His character and love. There are those of you who are waiting for much more than health insurance, a job, and a spouse. Some of you are waiting for an answer to the cancer diagnosis, a kidney transplant, the ability to find relief from daily chronic pain, for your spouse to leave his mistress and return to you, for your child to come back home, for the chemo treatment to work...the list goes on and on. The weight of wait bears down on your shoulders, and you hold your breath while hoping for the best. Sleepless nights, tearful mornings, and tasteless appetite-lacking lunches accumulate into months and years. It's hard to chalk it all up to a God who cares and is willing to give us more than we can ask or imagine.

In these moments of waiting, questioning, searching, or restlessness, God is not concerned with giving us "the answer" or the ending. Many times, that won't be revealed until the fulfillment actually takes place, or it may never be fulfilled until the other side of this life. God is more concerned with the journey. The point is this: It's not about the result, it's about the wrestling. That's where God comes and meets us, even though it often feels as though He is literally light years away. God wants us to live in the discomfort. God wants us to limp from the wrestle. God wants us to sit in the silence. There are things you learn by just "being," and things we gain when we find ourselves stuck. This is where transformation takes place— one miserable day after the other. God knows that in our humanity, if we had the ability, we'd speed up the clock and rush through the pain so we would feel only a slight pinch, and hurry to cross off lessons on the "to-do" list. If we had the ability to learn the lesson without the discomfort, we would certainly choose to audit that class and just read the CliffsNotes. Oh, God knows us so well! And this realization always makes me mad at first, like a caged cat—hissing and clawing.

Feeling trapped in a season or situation I don't like—and then I'm left grateful. When God protects us despite ourselves, that's mercy! When God doesn't let us receive what we long for without first having our longings met in Him, that's love! When God lets you sit in your humanity and act in your humanity yet never lets you leave His sovereignty, that's grace!

How so? We look to Christ. If God would not spare even His own son from discomfort, pain, and longing, then how much more would He also not permit us access to the same suffering? Being stuck begets suffering, suffering begets brokenness, brokenness begets humility, and humility begets intimacy. And intimacy with Christ begets transformation.

> Dear friends, do not be surprised at the fiery ordeal that has come on you to test you, as though something strange were happening to you. But rejoice inasmuch as you participate in the sufferings of Christ, so that you may be overjoyed when his glory is revealed. If you are insulted because of the name of Christ, you are blessed, for the Spirit of glory and of God rests on you. (1 Peter 4:12–14)

Although this passage speaks about the suffering of persecution, it reveals that there is something about suffering that is close to the heart of God. God is pruning away the familiarities of this life to make room for new growth.

> Endure hardship as discipline; God is treating you as his children. For what children are not disciplined by their father? If you are not disciplined—and everyone undergoes discipline—then you are not legitimate, not true sons and daughters at all. Moreover, we

have all had human fathers who disciplined us and we respected them for it. How much more should we submit to the Father of spirits and live! They disciplined us for a little while as they thought best; but God disciplines us for our good, in order that we may share in his holiness. No discipline seems pleasant at the time, but painful. Later on, however, it produces a harvest of righteousness and peace for those who have been trained by it.

And we boast in the hope of the glory of God. Not only so, but we also glory in our sufferings, because we know that suffering produces perseverance; perseverance, character; and character, hope. And hope does not put us to shame, because God's love has been poured out into our hearts through the Holy Spirit, who has been given to us. (Romans 5:2b–5)

Sometimes, I must confess, it didn't bring me much comfort to know that all the waiting and angst that surrounded the struggle was for the development of my character. It didn't seem like a good enough answer. What did bring me comfort, however, was the fact that our God is one who empathizes with our pain. "For we do not have a high priest who is unable to empathize with our weaknesses, but we have one who has been tempted in every way, just as we are—yet he did not sin. Let us then approach God's throne of grace with confidence, so that we may receive mercy and find grace to help us in our time of need" (Hebrews 4:14–16). We do not have to suffer alone. Pity the one who must traverse these hardships without the knowledge or recognition that the Great Comforter is available and near to those who believe. But blessed is the one who reaches for the hand of the greatest Companion, the One who promises to bring good from it all. The Divine is well-acquainted with pain. "The LORD is close to the brokenhearted and saves those who are crushed in spirit" (Psalm 34:18).

For 430 years, the Israelites were stuck in captivity in Egypt and oppressively held under Pharaoh's control. Called by God, Moses, knowing that God was behind the whole crazy plan, made request after request for Pharaoh to release the Israelites from their imprisoned servitude. Pharaoh's heart was hardened; despite the multiple plagues, he still would not let go. Meanwhile, the Israelites were subject to hardship, death, disease, and brutality as they waited for freedom. But our relentless God worked through Moses, Aaron, and every plague to finally break the bondage Pharaoh held over the Israelites. "During the night Pharaoh summoned Moses and Aaron and said, 'Up! Leave my people, you and the Israelites! Go, worship the LORD as you have requested'" (Exodus 12: 31). Sometimes God does His most wondrous works in the darkest of night.

So the Israelites left. They ran. They fled, and the sea was parted. God was driving their freedom and the wait appeared to be over. But something happened. God did not free them so that freedom would be found apart from Him. "When Pharaoh let the people go, God did not lead them on the road through the Philistine country, though that way was shorter. For God said, "If they face war, they might change their minds and return to Egypt" (Exodus 13:17–18). Like a good parent, God knew His children. And what should have been an 11-day journey turned into forty years of "stuck-ness" in the wilderness. The people of God were slaves to a godless nation. They had four hundred and thirty years of sin, bondage, and brokenness that needed to be reclaimed and restored. They were not yet ready to inhabit the Promised Land, because they didn't know how to find dependence on their God. During their years in the wilderness, we watch the Israelites attempt to retreat to a place of slavery because they're so unfamiliar with freedom. They were so uncomfortable with being stuck and had such a repulsive distaste for waiting for the promise that they preferred to suffer and sin in the wilderness. Although they were in the process of being freed, they were not yet delivered.

Despite their sin trapping them in the desert, God did not waste the apparently superfluous time in the wilderness. He used that time to strip away the sins of their hearts and the idols in their lives. He taught them about provision, lordship, and trust. In the waiting, His faithfulness and glory were experienced and not just pondered as a religious ideology. Ultimately, He transformed them from slave laborers to Promised Land inheritors.

I'm not suggesting that your season of being stuck is due to sin or that it's even prolonged by stubbornness, like that of the Israelites. If that's the case, I trust that God will reveal it to you in the proper place and at the proper time. I am suggesting, however, that God is purposeful even when you feel as though you are trapped in the wilderness. If you're in a season of waiting, be encouraged: God is not wasting your time. Seek His leading more than your longings, and when you find yourself circling in the desert land, stop and rest in His trustworthiness. Don't hasten the discomfort—sit and stay awhile. Learn what the stillness bears. God is moving, as the earth is rotating, so placidly that it's unnoticeable. But every morning, there's a new dawn rising.

Chapter 3

Shoulda, Coulda, Woulda

There are the things you know, and then there are the things you practice. Someone gives you a gift on your birthday, and you say "thank you." That is the correct response, so you practice it. Some older man with a walker is about to tread through the door. You know you should hold the door open as he passes by, so you do it. You see a child about to grab the boiling pot of water from the stove. To protect the tiny fingers from third-degree burns, you sweep in and scoop up the little one in your arms. Often, you know the right thing to do, and you act on it.

But then there are the times when you know what the right thing to do is, and you blow it. Someone cuts you off in traffic, so you ride their tail until the next exit. Your coworker asks you to help out and finish the job, but you choose to let him do the overtime because you just aren't in the mood to work extra. You get mad at your spouse for the offensive comment that cut your heart, so instead of being assertive or offering grace, you draw your own sword and stab back. It's a letdown after you realize what you did and what you *should* have done.

Why can't we just desire to want to do the right thing? Why is there always a daily dilemma? *This* is what I "should" do, but *that* is what I really "want" to do. Maybe we expect too much of ourselves. Perhaps we place a certain pressure on ourselves to be some sort of fairytale-perfect super person who does everything willingly and joyfully, and does it well. Instead, we're in this constant state of tension, sorting the "oughts" and the "should haves" from the "needs" and "I just can'ts."

There are times when you know you should have done better, when the opportunity was there but the moment missed. It's in those moments, when you become honest with yourself, that you see your motivation and your hidden agenda. You try to deny it, but the truth is evident—you are who you are, whether that be good or bad. Jesus once told Peter that "the spirit is willing, but the body is weak" (Matthew 26:41). How true those words are! We preach peace. We believe truthfulness is the best answer. We promote charity and generosity. We challenge people to spend time in devotions. We claim that Jesus has the answers to all the world's problems, and then...we live. We practice who we truly are instead of who we should be.

Now, I don't want us to be too hard on ourselves. I do believe with all my heart that we have a God big enough to handle our humanity. He sees our vile days as well as our sacred moments, and He loves us just the same regardless. He stands ready and waiting to forgive and to move us forward when our hearts act in repentance. I think it's the devil's trap to tell us that we aren't forgiven—to kick us when we're already down.

I'm convinced that there is a difference between guilt and conviction. To me, the lines get fuzzy, but I know that there is a difference. There is a conviction from God and a false guilt from the devil. False guilt tells us what a horrible person we are for doing such a horrible thing. It concentrates on the negative aspects of the situation and of our personhood. False guilt attacks our character and overemphasizes the weight of the offense. It looms over us like a stranger enticing a child with candy and persuades us that we can, in fact, be superhuman. When we fail, we get down on ourselves because we haven't achieved all that we were expected to. These are lies that I've believed and continue to struggle with. Just because I couldn't make (or even wanted to go to) the party to which I was invited, that doesn't mean I'm a bad person or a failure as a friend. Just because I didn't say "yes" and actually (for once) said "no" to something, that doesn't mean I rejected the person who asked. It means that I understand my limitations and know what my mind and body can handle. These lies, though, can choke us like a cord around the neck—cutting off the life within us until we become more delusional about who we really are. The situation becomes blown out of proportion, like a Barbie doll, until we reach the point where we don't know what to believe about ourselves.

[True conviction makes us want to be better. God's kindness leads us to repentance (Romans 2:4). It makes us acknowledge that there's a path that's more beautiful, more wholesome, and healthier. God illuminates another path, a better way. He reveals the next step. He doesn't overwhelm us with what we should be, nor does He degrade us by acknowledging who we could have been. Instead, He reminds of us of who we are meant to be and grants us the courage to say "yes" to that vision by making life-giving choices] This sounds simple and makes perfect sense when I explain it, but when push comes to shove, the true-and-false guilt becomes a medley of chaos in my brain. Quickly, I can find myself mulling over a decision, chewing on the situation like a piece of grizzled steak that's been in my mouth too long. It becomes nasty and nauseating. What I should have done, what I did—what was right? What was wrong? What should I do now? Stop. Relax. I can drive myself crazy just thinking about it.

We don't need to be superhuman, nor can we ever achieve perfection, which is an elusive goal. The greatest commandment Jesus left for us deals with love and not performance. "'Teacher, which is the greatest commandment in the Law?' Jesus replied: 'Love the Lord your God with all your heart and with all your soul and with all your mind. This is the first and greatest commandment. And the second is like it: Love your neighbor as yourself'" (Matthew 22:36–38). Although this commandment is lived out in both feelings and actions, Jesus is not handing us a load that we can't carry or a task that we can't achieve. He isn't making a list of things for us to do just right and to accomplish perfectly. This commandment requires that we love ourselves, too (Love your neighbor as *yourself*), which means that we can afford some grace for our own lives as well.

Superhuman perfection is often promoted in American culture as a form of success. While society subtly entices us to believe that achievement is found by balancing more and by saying "no" to less, the way of God is somewhat counterintuitive. Our finiteness is a part of the glory of God's infiniteness. For in our weakness, His strength is made known (2 Corinthians 12:10). Although we believe that we should live a certain way and that it's noble to aspire toward a proper way of living, we can get caught up in the expectations that we, the Church, and society place on ourselves. Often, these self-expectations are heavier and more burdensome than the expectations God places on us. Why? Because we, along with the rest of the world, attempt the impossible through our own strength. God, on the other hand, achieves the impossible in our lives through the source and strength of His Spirit working in us.

In Matthew 14 we see the humanity of Christ empowered and strengthened by the power of the Father. Jesus had just learned that his second cousin and a supporter of His ministry, John the Baptist, was heinously murdered through a beheading. Can you imagine the grief and sadness that Jesus must have felt? He not only lost someone He loved, but the person he loved was killed in a gruesome manner. Matthew 14:13 recounts that, "When Jesus heard what had happened, he withdrew by boat privately to a solitary place." With the weight of the burdensome news, Jesus retreated to a place of emotional and physical rest with His Father. And what a good thing He did, because as soon as His boat landed, He did not simply get off and walk home. He was greeted by a crowd of five thousand sick and needy people who followed Him to His remote destination—whining, begging, and desperate for food and healing. Like good friends do, the disciples attempted to release Jesus from the burden of tending to the crowd. They told Him, "This is a remote place, and it's already getting late. Send the crowds away, so they can go to the villages and buy themselves some food" (Matthew 14:15). But Jesus was so moved by compassion for the crowd that He began to heal and feed them. He couldn't say "no" but not because He felt obligated or was trying to appease society's definition of success. The reason He couldn't say no was because He was empowered by God. He was not operating on His own human strength; He was leaning on the power of the One who met Him in the solitary place to fill His spirit. Christ's reliance on God the Father empowered Him to perform a miracle of faith that evening. Despite the tragic news, despite His grief, despite His emotional and physical exhaustion, Christ, by the power imparted to Him by God, managed to take two fish and five loaves of bread to feed the crowd. "They all ate and were satisfied, and the disciples picked up twelve basketfuls of broken pieces that were left over" (Matthew 14:20). When we stop getting down on ourselves for the failure to meet the superhuman expectations we place on ourselves and start allowing our superhuman God to fill our spirit, the beneficial results can be exponential.

You may not be the mom of six kids who always has a clean house, has clothes pressed and folded, packs lunches with one serving of vegetables, one serving of fruit, and sliced wheat bread with low-sodium turkey, exercises two hours in the morning, helps at the local food bank, works forty hours plus overtime, and takes night classes just for fun while managing to set aside time for a nightly back massage for her husband after the five-course meal she has just prepared. And maybe you're unable to be the dad who works two full-time jobs, leads a Bible study, maintains the lawn like a golf course, helps his wife out with dinner, makes time to hunt, fish, and play football and baseball with his sons as he prepares for a 26-mile marathon and still manages to find time to massage his wife's feet at the end of each day. That's okay, and perhaps, in a sense, it's actually God-honoring. Every time we say "yes" to one thing, we by default are saying "no" to another. When I agree to foster a friendship by going out to coffee one evening during the week, I may be saying "no" to spending quality time with my husband and kids. When I agree to take additional college classes to further my education, I may be saying "no" to time spent on other important activities. To every "yes," there is a "no." Sometimes, it feels like a double-bind, but you must assess the "no" to determine if the cost is worth the benefit. There are many opportunities that are good and healthy, but what must always remain in our minds are the expectations God has placed on us. Do not run after whatever it is that you think society has planned for you. "Seek first his kingdom and his righteousness, and all these things will be given to you as well" (Matthew 6:33).

Are your expectations for yourself higher than God's expectations of you? It may be hard to believe, but when you expect more from yourself than what God expects of you, you have actually usurped the throne of God. You've made yourself the ultimate judge. There's a fine line between objectively looking at your personal shortcomings and critically assessing yourself to the point of self-degradation. Repentance leads to life, while hypercriticism leads to destruction. We weren't meant to be superhuman. We were meant to be humans loved by a super God. This is where faith comes in. In Romans, the Apostle Paul speaks about the frustrating tension of knowing how you ought to live but being confronted with your limitations.

> So I find this law at work: Although I want to do good, evil is right there with me. For in my inner being I delight in God's law; but I see another law at work in me, waging war against the law of my mind and making me a prisoner of the law of sin at work within me. What a wretched man I am! Who will rescue me from this body that

is subject to death? Thanks be to God, who delivers me through Jesus Christ our Lord! So then, I myself in my mind am a slave to God's law, but in my sinful nature a slave to the law of sin. (Romans 7:21–25)

The point is, we can't do it alone. We weren't meant to. We can't balance it all, we can't tirelessly run the race without running ourselves down first, we can't live like Christ and keep the world happy, we can't model perfection...it's all impossible apart from God. It takes faith and interdependence on His strength. It takes His love to illuminate the next most important task. It takes risk to say "no" to the other good options so that we make room for the best choice. It is resting, relying, submitting, and yielding...conforming to our loving God, first, with every ounce of our volition. When I allow God to fill me, just like Jesus filled the crowd with the fish and loaves, He can bring plenty from nothing. It was Christ who had to save us from our sins on the cross two thousand years ago. How much more is He still saving us from ourselves as we stumble around in our new robes of righteousness?

It's healthy to be honest with ourselves, our limitations, our dos and don'ts. But we need to stop listening to the false-guilt lies of the devil, who tries to convince us that what we do is who we are. The shoulds and oughts will work themselves out if we make it our priority to love God with all our being. Honesty before God and repentance will always eventually bring you to the place you need to be...dependent on God's strength rather than your own. Let God be the superhuman hero. After all, He is the Savior in this story we call life.

Chapter 4

The Table Holds More Than Food

Grandma's house is a magical place, not just from my perspective as a child—the magic remains way into adulthood. I've been blessed with the world's best grandma. I know everyone says that, but mine is extra special. She's a cute little thing, measuring, on a good day, four feet nine inches. I'm anything but what you would call "tall," but put a pair of shoes on me, and I tower over Grandma. Grandma means so much to our family, and does so much for us. She became a Christian at age 16 after her mother passed away, and her father was a far cry from what a father is supposed to be. She was the only one in her family who was a believer, and for years she was persecuted for her faith by those close to her. She met my wonderful grandpa, and they married and had my uncle and my mom, who made their own decisions to adopt the faith of my grandparents. I have great admiration for my grandmother's commitment and perseverance in following Jesus when she had so many reasons to give up and to turn bitter. God had always been her first love—that's very obvious in the way she lives her life. Our family calls her our "prayer warrior." Grandma probably has permanent imprints on her knees from years of kneeling in prayer for our family and for others. She's the woman who gets up early just so that she can pray an hour for her family's safety and protection as they drive to work each morning. She's a beautiful example of a woman humbled before the Lord.

When I was little, Grandma used to play with me using all the imaginary scenarios I would conjure up—dress-up, pretending I was the owner of a restaurant or store, or acting as if I were married and had babies. As soon as I would walk through Grandma's door, I would start to play, making so many fun memories at her place. As I grew older and the toys vanished, Grandma began to share a bit of her talents with me. She's taught me how to crochet, which, sadly, the student—not the teacher—has failed at repeatedly. I can't seem to get past the chain or the square. I would love to, at some point in my life, actually complete a blanket, but I've been working on the same pink, yarn square for almost a decade now. She's taught me how to make throws and use a sewing machine. Surprisingly, I have not sewn my fingers together (although I've come close many times). I have a lead foot when I drive, and I handle the sewing machine pedal with the same gumption. It takes off like a car fleeing a bank robbery, and Grandma just laughs. She's tried to teach me patience, but that might be another unattainable goal. She's taught me how to make homemade applesauce, homemade pie crust, and how to decorate a cake. She attempted to teach me, via a long-distance phone call, how to make her famous chicken and gravy. I kept asking what color the gravy should be, and if I put too much butter or flour in it. Through the phone, she guided me and encouraged me to keep tending to it, although it was developing into a color and consistency that was different from her normal gravy. That evening, around three a.m., I woke up to what seemed to be a gallbladder attack and realized that I'd screwed something up in the recipe. I knew it wasn't the same as hers, despite my valiant efforts.

My grandma and mom are the world's greatest cooks. I've got some big shoes to fill, and I have the best chefs to teach me. They whip stuff up like it was nothing—they make it seem so effortless. Each time you take a bite, a taste of Heaven overwhelms your taste buds. I swear I don't quite know how the food in Heaven can ever top the food I've tasted here. Maybe that will be their jobs in Heaven.

There's a little round table in Grandma's kitchen, and every time I enter her house, as sure as the sun sets, there's some sort of delicious food on that table and waiting to be consumed... by me (if the rest of the family is lucky, I'll share.) Oh, I love that table. It has held peach pie, apple pie, strawberry double-crusted pie, rhubarb pie, apple dumplings, chocolate chip cookies, brownies, frosted cut-out cookies, chocolate-covered pretzels, homemade rolls, chocolate-covered peanuts, cornbread, homemade cinnamon rolls, chocolate cake, vanilla cake with homemade frosting, mallow cups, Texas chocolate sheet cake, no-bakes—oh...and napkins! Our family loves food, and for any celebratory or even non-celebratory meal, we hold to the conviction that a main course, appetizer, and side dish just simply aren't enough.

Food isn't wonderful just because it's food. There is so much more to a meal than just what is being consumed. It's the fellowship, the tradition, the love, and community that take place around the table. I hear people talk about diets, and my first thought is, "Wow, that takes so much self-discipline. I don't know if I'd be strong enough." How do you pass up a donut or a chocolate chip cookie? It's like turning down an innocent child who just wants to be held. Such internal turmoil, it's not even funny. My second thought is to encourage the dieter by saying, "Don't do it!" in sheer desperation, as if they were getting ready to pull the trigger. (Guess I'm not a very good accountability partner). And my third thought is that there's so much more they are missing than just the food. That's why diets are so hard. Food is a symbol of love, nourishment, and community. Around the dinner table are the faces of the ones you love, the laughter over stories, old and new, and the enjoyment of sharing common interests and experiences. It's a time to know and to be known. It's intimate and personal. Not everyone is invited to dinner. It's not an event that is all-inclusive to strangers and neighbors. It's an event that you share with those you invite, those you long to learn more about and be near to, and whose company you'll be enriched by. That's why a couple goes out to eat, just he and she, at a small table for two. The rest of the world hums and buzzes around them, but at their small table for two, they are engaging in something much deeper than the aroma of the entrée and the luscious bite of dessert. They are talking, laughing, and sharing, and for one split second, everything seems all right in the world.

While growing up, my parents always made sure we ate dinner together every night during the week. It was all I ever knew, and it was so healthy for us as a family. It gave us time to unwind from the day, communicate with each other, share stories, both good and bad, and discover what was going on in each other's lives. I looked forward to it, and even now I carry on this tradition with my husband. It's something that we both value and make an effort to maintain. A sense of belonging and acceptance can be found at the dinner table. Statistics have proven that families are happier when they eat together. Below are two statistics from studies performed by The National Center on Addiction and Substance Abuse (CASA) at Columbia University:

The family dinners report found that teens having frequent family dinners are more likely to report having excellent relationships with their family members. Compared to teens having infrequent family dinners, teens having frequent family dinners are

-one and a half times more likely to report having an excellent relationship with their mothers;

-more than twice as likely to report having an excellent relationship with their fathers;

-almost twice as likely to report having an excellent relationship with their sibling(s).

Compared to teens who have frequent family dinners (five to seven per week), those who have infrequent family dinners (fewer than three per week) are almost *four times likelier to use tobacco, more than twice as likely to use alcohol, two and a half times likelier to use marijuana, and almost four times more likely to say they expect to try drugs in the future,* according to the The Importance of Family Dinners VII (CASA Columbia, 2011).5

I want to continue family mealtimes with my own children. I want to make them food and for all of us to gather around the table in the evening to discuss life and the day's events, no matter how tired or grouchy we may feel. The important thing is that we have each other, every night. Even if the rest of the world is falling apart, we have each other. And that in itself is worth a toast.

There is so much more to cooking than adding a half cup of this with a tablespoon of that: whisk, pour, and bake at 350 degrees.

Cooking, I believe, is an art form. Even the unskilled can follow a simple recipe and create. You can add your own flair, tweak the recipe, or create something from scratch. It's a way of expressing yourself—what you like, something new, something old, and producing aesthetic appeal. Cooking equals creation—a beautiful creation that offers fulfillment, nourishment, and flavor. I want to cook, not just so my husband will have something to eat but to carry on the family traditions of love and fellowship. I want to be the woman who can mix up anything in a pinch if someone's stomach is growling and the woman who always has something warm and yummy sitting on the counter to share with her loved ones. My kitchen and I have made a couple of fun meals together. I have a blue and white apron I *must* wear when cooking. That apron is no ordinary apron, either. It has special meaning because it was made by the same grandma who passed down so many of her unsurpassed skills to me. I have hosted friends and family on occasions that have been so fulfilling and rewarding and have allowed me to experience times of fellowship and communing that I never want to forget. I remember the importance food had to me during a time I was depressed by events that had occurred in my life. Everything seemed so miserable, but I remember thinking, *Even if everything else sucks, at least food tastes good.* Many Tuesday nights in the past, I have gathered with some of my closest friends to eat a home-cooked meal. Each week we'd trade houses, taking turns to host. Those Tuesday nights were moments of pure joy during sometimes difficult, or even easy, weeks. We'd share stories and complaints about life, knowing that every Tuesday night came with a guarantee of a good time. We girls would be entertained by the guys' Will Ferrell-like misbehavior. Sometimes we'd all laugh so hard we'd cry, soon developing inside jokes and ridiculous nicknames for one another. And although I've had to move away from those beautiful friends, we still maintain a closeness and connection, and are inseparable despite the miles between us.

Jesus, in the book of Revelation, is talking to the Laodicean church. This church was known to have become lukewarm—neither on fire for God nor completely hating God. They were sitting apathetically in the middle and living lives unchanged and unmoved by the Almighty, Creator, living God. Jesus calls them to repentance and says, "Here I am! I stand at the door and knock. If anyone hears my voice and opens the door, I will come in and eat with that person, and they with me" (Revelation 3:20). I find it interesting that Jesus uses the imagery of a meal when describing His desire to be in proper communion with the Laodicean church. He doesn't say, "Come, and I will walk with you" or "Come, and I will work with you." He says, "I will come in and eat with that person and they with me." I believe that's significant. To Jesus, a meal isn't just a meal; it's a time for close, personal communion. It's a time when strangers are no longer strangers but instead a venue in which the walls come down and connections are made. The table is a place to be fed physically and spiritually. It's a place to be refreshed and re-energized. Jesus didn't want the Laodiceans to know Him as a distant king. He wanted to dine with them as if He were a family member or a best friend. He longed to be a part of their community and to have them be a part of His loving fellowship.

Sometimes I think it's easy to forget that the God who can often seem either too distant or too majestic just longs to sit with us in such a way that it mirrors the fellowship, laughter, and acceptance that is found around the table. Have you ever wondered if He set a place for you? This is the uniqueness found within Christianity that makes it unlike all other religions. This God condescends. By that, I mean He took it upon himself to leave the throne and to invite people into fellowship with Him. This God prepared the table. This God made the first move.

Food is such a staple in our lives. It's necessary for us to take time out to eat, something for which I'm thankful. I've shared countless meals with precious friends. I can picture their faces now and even still hear some of their conversations lingering in the depths of my memory. A tribute to you and to your hearts, dear friends—a toast to the ways you filled my soul, far more than the meal we shared. Let us raise our glasses to the holy One who dines with sinners and knocks patiently, waiting for us to invite Him closer. May we be reminded that food is so much more than food: It's the fellowship of kindred souls.

Chapter 5

In the Presence

There is a power in just "being." There is a comfort in being in the presence of someone, even if no words are spoken. There is a comfort in a hand-to-hand connection. There is an unexplained beauty in silence. I'm not usually one prone to enjoying silence. Silence usually results in rising internal tension...but now, I'm beginning to see the power behind the unspoken.

I don't think we always have to have an answer. We don't always have to have a response or say what we are thinking. To accept and rest in what is received is a simple yet deep blessing. I struggle with the pressure of always needing to react and to spend much energy attempting to meet the unseen expectations I subconsciously assume are being placed upon me by others.

I have talked so much that I have become numb to my own voice. I love words and expressing all that I'm feeling, and sometimes expression is best when left sealed in the restful recesses of the soul. I have cried my way to the heart of God only to find my puddle of tears and the deafness of the air surrounding me—I've cried so loud, I couldn't hear the gentle voice of my Comforter.

Tonight, I spent time simply "being" with someone I love dearly. I did not perform. I did not strive. I did not entertain. I did not expect. I did not plan. I sat. I dwelt. I enjoyed. I lived in the moment. And the moment wasn't that grand or extraordinary. It didn't offer new inspiration. It wasn't efficient or productive. I gained very little, but yet I gained much. I sat in the "presence," and that in itself was profound. I'm not used to doing something without using it as a means to cross an item off my "to-do" list. It feels wasteful. But tonight wasn't wasteful. Tonight, the ordinary was met by the Divine because there was space for Him to come.

I don't believe we were meant to be this busy. We were not built to distract ourselves with noises, obligations, and pressures that minimize the space within which we hear the gentle Spirit. We fall beautifully into the trap of our Enemy. He says, *Keep going, there is so much to do, there are so many people to make happy, there are so many goals to meet, there's more money you need for the bills, go, go, go....* And so we go until we've beat down our bodies, our minds, and our spirit... exhausted, depleted, and terribly distracted. Then we wonder why we can't hear God. It's difficult to hear when the clattering of everything else reverberates around us. In our society, wearing many hats is highly regarded and is expected. If you don't do it all, you look like a failure, a weak person. Just the angst of having the stigma of a wimp is enough to push yourself into overdrive. The risk of looking worse than your neighbor, your boss, your best friend, your sister...is all too great. Saying "no" is really not an option—too much could be lost. Loss of approval, loss of a friendship, loss of peace, loss of a job—there's too much at stake.

I suppose that if one wants to truly encounter the Divine, some sort of loss must occur. Because God won't force His way into a place that has no room for Him. Sometimes you must wait in the presence. And the presence may not be in the grandeur but rather in the simplicity of it all.

> The LORD said, "Go out and stand on the mountain in the presence of the LORD, for the LORD is about to pass by." Then a

great and powerful wind tore the mountains apart and shattered the rocks before the LORD, but the LORD was not in the wind. After the wind there was an earthquake, but the LORD was not in the earthquake. After the earthquake came a fire, but the LORD was not in the fire. And after the fire came a gentle whisper. When Elijah heard it, he pulled his cloak over his face and went out and stood at the mouth of the cave. (1 Kings 19:11–13)

Oh, the simplicity and intimacy of a whisper—the presence in the unexpected.

I'm sure that you, like everyone else, feel busier than you can handle, but please rest. God beckons you to rest. Sit in silence. Turn down the music. Hear the unwelcomed crickets. Feel the weight of the silence. Stop talking and receive. Sit, dwell...be, just be. It's okay. It's okay to say no, to slow down and stop...it's very good. The God who has been gently whispering longs for your presence as you abide in His presence. Just "be" with a loved one. Just sit in the same room with them. Just knowing you are there fills an indefinable need of the heart. Be grateful for the opportunity. Productivity and efficiency are not always the goals to be achieved. Sometimes the greatest goal to be achieved is not even a goal at all—it is an appreciation of the moment at hand. Tear up the agenda, forfeit the distractions and become awakened to the ordinary around you. Be in the presence.

Chapter 6

"ings" not "eds"

I don't quite understand the mystery of the misfiring neurons. Maybe it's just a mislabeled heavenly postage package. Like the carrier is still traversing the course set forth from head to heart. It's discouraging sometimes. Like you can touch it but you can't feel it. Like you can eat it but not taste it. Missing pieces, disconnected, asking but not receiving. There are things you learn, things you hear and "get," truths you know. And that's where it remains—in the receiving dock and ready to be shipped, but it doesn't manage to meet its destination of the heart. Trapped in the mind, lost in transit. And there sits the heart like a mother looking at her premature newborn inside an incubator—so near, yet not able to hold. So she yearns, she grasps, she waits, she aches, she prays, she hopes, she mourns...ah, the torment of the "so close, but out of reach."

I have found in the past that I thought I truly knew and understood something, some important truths of the gospel. Years passed by, blinders were removed from my eyes, and the clouds parted only to reveal...I totally didn't get it at all. It was kind of like the time when I finally realized that Hawaii was *not* located off the coast of Florida. Took until high school to uncover that one. All those years, I could have sworn you just jumped on a ship and sailed off the sandy beaches of the Sunshine State into the tropical bliss of Hawaii. (A little west, my dear.) Slightly shocking. However, the Hawaii mix-up is still a little different. That is a confusion of facts. I'm talking about a confusion between understanding something in your head and understanding something in your heart. I have come to realize that there is a large chasm that lies between knowing something and internalizing it. And so my internal security guard checks those thoughts twice. *Do I really believe this? Is this just a nice tidy picture of what I believe as truth, or is this something I understand deep in the core of my being?*

I don't claim to know much, but one thing I do know is that it's essential to ask yourself the hard questions. You can blind yourself for years, and you can choose to look the other way. You can choose to ignore internal incongruities and brush them under a rug like dirt. But motives, agendas, and blindness remain. The best thing you can do to love yourself, love others, love life, and love God is to be honest, first and foremost with yourself.

I'm so grateful to my parents for many of the life lessons they taught me, but one of the most powerful values they imparted was the importance of honesty. My mom always told me that I would get into less trouble if I told the truth rather than telling a lie. Good deal. And so I always told the truth, even if that meant I got in trouble. And on the rare occasions when I attempted to slide away from being truthful, watch out! Mom wasn't kidding. I'm grateful for their consistency in not only modeling honest lives, but for continually reminding me the worth of such a virtue—that is a priceless gift. The rest of your possessions can be taken from you, but not your honesty. And in the honesty, that's where God meets us—in the honesty of the brokenness, in the honesty of the loneliness, in the honesty of the waiting, in the honesty of hoping...in the honesty of the soul search.

It is to your own detriment when you lie to yourself. You start losing ground, spending more time deciding between reality and facade. In the mesh of it all you lose who you are and what you're about. Fact is, if you can't be honest with yourself, then you can't be honest with anybody else. More importantly, you can't be honest with God. And when you can't be honest with God, you block yourself from the source of healing and love.

So now, here I sit in the honesty of it all, laying it all out on the table before God only to find...I don't get it! The love of God has gotten lost in transit. For me, I have found that it is easier to love God than to truly know He loves me. I know in my head He loves me. Yes, yes, "Jesus loves me this I know..." I've sung the song a million times, along with the rest of the population. I know it's true. "For God so loved the world..." John 3:16. One the of the few Bible verses I've memorized. Got it. Heard, read, and recited it a thousand times, too. All my neurons are on board for that. But my heart?? What happened? Why does my heart remain unmoved? Why does His love feel so distant? Why does a smile from a stranger stir me more than a familiar Bible verse? And this is when honesty is difficult.

I know I should understand the love of God. I see it all around me. He protects me, He forgives me, He provides for me, He comforts me, He helps me...it's all around. So here I am swimming right in the middle of God's pool of love, totally immersed and yet completely dry. I don't feel any of it. What more does He have to do? After all, He gave me His life. You'd think that would be enough to set my heart ablaze, but I'm left flatlined.

Look around—it appears that most of us do walk around unemotive to the love of God. A pair of jeans that on sale for the lovely markdown price of $10.99 or a new sports car with impressive torque excites us more than the fact that the One who created, I don't know, like maybe…THE GALAXIES and everything within, happens to have more than just a mild interest in us. That should be mind-blowing. That should be soul-soaring. That should be propelling us to live alive and not apathetically. But here we go…on and about our daily mundane tasks, afraid to know this God any deeper than a Sunday morning connection because—heaven forbid—He might require something of us.

It's frustrating to me to know that I should be captivated by this love but yet not feel it. It's like seeing a building but you can't get there. You know where you should be. You can even see the destination, but you have a bunch of one-way streets and unfamiliar road signs that detour your path. I just want to "get it," to be truly and fully captivated and overcome by the love of God. I know it would change me and how I live and how I love. I know I would find more value in myself because I'm no longer a "no-name" who determines my worth from the approval of others or the lack thereof. I would see myself and know myself as one who is deeply loved, one who is completely known…one who belongs.

I love God—I love Him deeply. That seems so much easier. It feels more natural for me to love Him back. All that He does—His sovereignty, His protection, His provision, His omnipotence—makes my heart sincerely overflow with love and gratitude. But I guess I treat him like a famous musician. I can love that musician for the music they play, the lyrics they write, the way their songs inspire my heart, but to them, I am just another face in the crowd, a fan whom they appreciate but don't know personally. I'm there, and they're glad that I'm there, but they don't know me. They don't know that I'm addicted to chocolate. They don't know I love sleeping in on Saturdays. They don't know that I love science but hate math. I love Him for Him, but I can't get how He loves me for me.

Matters of the mind that aren't resolved remain unsettled in my soul. I can't just let them go, which honestly would be a relief sometimes. If only I could just pack up this not-so-nice realization in a box and store it in the attic for a couple decades, until it makes sense. Then I could go get it out again and enjoy what I learned. Wouldn't that be nice? But it doesn't work that way. There's a process and a wait. I don't like it. And I think that is right where God wants me. Sitting, searching, and desiring. Stuck in the "ings," not yet having made it to the "eds." I am "seeking" but have not "learned." I am "striving" but have not "grasped." I am "understanding" but have not "internalized." Like all lovers, God longs to be sought after. He wants to be pursued by us not for the gifts He gives but in the gift of who He is.

I have found myself praying a lot. Isaiah 55:8–11 says,

"For my thoughts are not your thoughts, neither are your ways my ways," declares the LORD. "As the heavens are higher than the earth, so are my ways higher than your ways and my thoughts than your thoughts. As the rain and the snow come down from heaven, and do not return to it without watering the earth and making it bud and flourish, so that it yields seed for the sower and bread for the eater so is my word that goes out from my mouth: It will not return to me empty, but will accomplish what I desire and achieve the purpose for which I sent it."

God says that His word won't return void. I'm betting on that. I don't know about you, but I think that out of all people in this universe, God is the one I can hold to His word. Practice the discipline of praying Scripture because God can use it for good in our hearts. Paul's prayer in Ephesians 3:18–19 is that we "may have power, together with all the Lord's holy people, to grasp how wide and long and high and deep is the love of Christ, and to know this love that surpasses knowledge—that I may be filled to the measure of all the fullness of God." It's time to know the love of God as deeply and intimately as Paul did. Mediocrity has lost its appeal.

I don't know what to expect, or when I'll finally be completely consumed by the understanding of God's love for me. I don't know how long I'll wait until my heart is no longer numb. All I've got to offer is my honesty. All I have to claim is my confession. But then maybe that's what it's all about. The love God has for me, for us, is so consuming, so fierce, so above-human, that it is just… incomprehensible, unexplainable, uncontainable, unable to be realized to its fullness. Perhaps that's the whole point—we should start the chase to uncover the immense love of God now and run after it into eternity.

Maybe we weren't meant to fully comprehend, because a fully comprehensible god would not be a god at all. Love is a mystery. God is love (1 John 4:18)—the author and embodiment of every complexity that love entails. Within God is mystery. The apostle Paul speaks frequently about this mystery:

> I have become its servant by the commission God gave me to present to you the word of God in its fullness— the mystery that has been kept hidden for ages and generations, but is now disclosed to the Lord's people. To them God has chosen to make known among the Gentiles the glorious riches of this mystery, which is Christ in you, the hope of glory. (Colossians 1:25–27)

> Pray also for me, that whenever I speak, words may be given me so that I will fearlessly make known the mystery of the gospel, for which I am an ambassador in chains. Pray that I may declare it fearlessly, as I should. (Ephesians 6:19–20)

The Greek word used for mystery is *mystērion*, which can be "summarized as knowledge and understanding in a spiritual sense of the life, death, and resurrection of Jesus the Christ. Learning and understanding of this mystery does not come via human intellectual or philosophical achievement. The only way to grasp it is through revelation from God."[6] The mystery of the love of God has been and continues to be revealed through the work of Christ on the cross. It is a revelation granted to us—an uncovering of the eyes, so to speak.

When Christ's death on the cross becomes no more than a familiar childhood Sunday school story, and His resurrection is photobombed by the latest Facebook feed, then we have quite possibly lost the appeal and intrigue of the greatest sacrifice made on our behalf. Something happened over two thousand years ago—something changed the course of history so much so that we record time relative to this event (AD-Anno Domini). There were, and are, "glorious riches" wrapped within this event. I don't think these riches can be simply summed up or understood but rather they unfold over time, in God's time.

We must find the balance—pursue God, yet wait for revelation. We must get real with our heart's lack of luster and ask God to open our eyes a little more to the mystery of His love. The more we seek, the more our hearts will be captivated by His grandeur. Then one day, on the other side of this finite life, when we enter His throne room, our heads will finally unite with our hearts, and God's glorious love will enrapture our entire being, the way it was always meant to. The "ings" will be "eds," and the race that was marked out before us will be worth the entire pursuit.

Chapter 7

The God-Box

I have a friend who stopped going to church years ago, keeps trying to find a church, but ends up disappointed and disconnected. I had another friend who, for the better half of two decades, had "church" with her devotional book, the Bible, and a pen. I had a coworker who never really agreed to the whole God thing and deemed himself an atheist because he thought God is egotistical and Christians are weaklings that use their religion as a crutch. There's another gal I know whose boyfriend's intellectual wanderings brought him to a place of atheism. One of my other friends says that God and he are pretty cool right now. He doesn't really go to church. He'd like to go, but between the hypocrites and the complacency, he just doesn't make it there. Then some other guy I know said that he tried being a good Christian, tried reading and praying and all those "Christiany" things, but they didn't work. One of my other friends loves spiritual things and believes in prayer and in living a peaceful life, but doesn't really hold to Jesus as the One and Only. Although I don't agree with them, I get where they are all coming from.

I used to have long life-talks with the "God and I are cool" friend during late-night drives. As we toured back roads and random towns, we would talk about God, questions, and frustrations. It was as raw and rich as a sip of dry red wine. We'd talk for hours, and maybe we didn't come up with answers to our questions, but somehow, we made progress in the search just by chewing over the topic for a while. Just as much as he'd hearten my spirit, I would his. After the "Hi, how are you's?" we'd bypass the superficial fluff and quickly delve into a deep conversation about God and our souls. You could tell that God was in the midst of those late night ventures. I learned and sorted through a lot of emotional junk in that '97 Jetta. I swear, a good conversation or two can sometimes be more powerful than a lecture from the pulpit. It isn't the sanctuary, neither is it the steering wheel that makes those moments so transforming. It's the God who comes and acts as the third party at the occasion.

I like to believe in a big God, not because it's a belief I decided to select when shopping at the "Store of Religions," but because it is a true thought. I used to have a small view of God. He was very capricious and often angry. He probably had a cane and an oversized head with a constant scowl, like some creepy wizard who could never be pleased. It took a few years of soul-searching, god-searching, and many small seeds of truth planted here and there, for me to finally overcome this small view of God.

I grew up in the Church. In general, there is a lot you learn about God, but more accurately, there seems to be a lot more you learn about being a "good Christian." You learn how to perfect the "goodie two shoes" image and how to reject those who are "sinners." You learn how to be a morally good person, how to properly interject clichés at a much unneeded moment, and how to gently tell those around that they're going to hell. And you are expected to go forth and share this all in the name of Jesus.

The church I grew up in served to do much more good for me than harm. I was taught sound doctrine (which seems to be a rare find these days), honesty, genuine love, and forgiveness. It also helped to form in me a deep passion for learning about God (even if He was like a mean old wizard with a cane). When I speak of the church, I'm making a generalization about the American community of churches. As my father would say, there is "the great bell curve of life." By that, he meant that there is a middle section in which the majority of people stand, and then there are the outliers on either side. Most churches in America lie in the camel's hump, the big upward curve in the middle. There are a few outlier churches that "get it," and then there are some churches that are so far away from teaching the truths of God that they might as well put a sign on their door that says, "Closed to God's truth, adhering to our own." But truly, does any church really "get it"? Aren't we all just a part of an ongoing conversation, sharpening each other by our differing interpretations?

In my conversations, experiences, and observations, I've found that Americans are becoming more and more disenchanted with church. And I think *who can blame them?* It feels as though American Christianity has become either a sitcom or a tragedy, and no matter the channel, it renders a sad array of cheap entertainment, offensive behaviors, and fluffy words. So many channels, yet nothing's really on.

I don't believe this was how it was supposed to be when Christ ascended and left Peter and the other apostles with the task of establishing the Church. When you read through the epistles, the letters Paul, John, James, and others wrote, there is this constant striving to correct false doctrines that were intermixing into true Christianity. This correction continued into the third century and throughout the canonization process. I think as the years have progressed and man's corruptions began permeating further into the gospel message, Christianity took on a new face. I'm becoming more convinced that American Christianity and its God have become so small that it's lost its appeal.

It grieves me to think about the reflection of Christ we project to the world. Have we become no greater than a community which enacts and imposes moral legislation? There seems to be a God-box—an understood list of rules and proper behavior that Christians are expected to exhibit. In this box, morality lines the borders, and God has been shrunk to fit inside. It almost becomes a form of idolatry: Worship the religion instead of the God of the religion. There is a hierarchy of sin in the God-box that seems to be very commonplace in American churches. There's the Christian top five of what not to do—don't drink, don't smoke, don't do drugs, don't swear, and don't have sex before marriage. If you abstain from these things, you are considered a God-fearing, good Christian. These five sins seem to be overly elevated above all the others. Why? What ever happened to gossip or slander? What about grumbling, idolatry, or greed? Did we forget about vanity or materialism? What about gluttony? Or more importantly, how about truly loving one another and not judging one another? Have we mastered that yet? And why is having a glass of wine taboo? I think of far worse things we ingest when making a quick stop at the Golden Arches.

The God-box mentality pushes people away. It creates an atmosphere of hypocritical judgment and pride. God-box followers become so obsessed with separation from sin that they begin to base their relationship with God totally on abstaining and overcoming sin. Then soon, their belief about sin-control becomes imposed upon outsiders to the point at which they start calling other people out on their sins. To them, it's a way of honoring a holy God. And even though they have good intentions of preserving the righteousness God calls us to, they end up hurting people deeply in the process of doing so. Rarely do I believe that it is our place to say something that calls someone out. God will deal with each in His own time. People are consumed with other people's moral behavior and spend more time picking the speck of dust out of their neighbor's eye while missing the plank that remains in their own. Paul says in Romans 2:1,

> You, therefore, have no excuse, you who pass judgment on someone else, for at whatever point you judge another, you are condemning yourself, because you who pass judgment do the same things. Now we know that God's judgment against those who do such things is based on truth. So when you, a mere human being, pass judgment on them and yet do the same things, do you think you will escape God's judgment? Or do you show contempt for the riches of his kindness, forbearance and patience, not realizing that God's kindness is intended to lead you to repentance?

Instead of pulling the "God-card" on people, I think we should be spending the effort in love and prayer. God can change their hearts sooner than our nitpicking. Let it rest in His hands. So much damage has been done all in the name of Christ, it's heartbreaking. And we can see degenerative results by the number of dying churches in America.

I'm not denying that sin needs to be dealt with, because look around for thirty seconds: the effects of sin are obviously exponential. I understand there are times when certain problems do need to be addressed. I once heard a pastor preach that it's actually unloving to *not* bring the blatant sin of your brother or sister in Christ to their attention, and this is true. Paul instructs in Galatians 6:1, "Brothers, if someone is caught in a sin, you who are spiritual should restore him gently." But notice how he adds the word "gently." It's important to note that blatant sin is very different than personal conviction. There are gray areas, and there are black and white areas in the Bible. There are personal convictions, and there are Christian liberties. There is a time to speak, and a time to refrain.

It is true that Christianity has too often become the extreme opposite. A man named Santa God just gives a small pat on the shoulder and turns a blind eye to the corruption and vileness spewing from the lifestyles of many casual Christians. Even Jesus talks about how much he hates lukewarm Christianity—He'd rather spit it out than partake of it (Revelation 3:16). If the church hasn't become a strict, fake, oppressive judicial system, then it seems to have become a corrupt politician promising wealth, health, and lax standards. Would the true face of the real gospel message please stand up?

Many people I've talked to don't find church to be a safe place. To them it's a location where you get stared at because of the way you're dressed, judged for your attitude, and reprimanded for your lifestyle. They are tired of the hypocrisy. A church that has arguments about simple, secondary matters such as music and attire, manages to always find a way to point the finger. Meanwhile, preachers who talk about the blood of Christ being the only thing that saves are caught having relations with a girl in the youth group. A group of so-called "holy ladies" gossip about another sister's language behind her back. Even men on television sell Jesus with color-coded Bibles claiming that with their gift of money they will receive a special Bible that possesses healing powers available to those who just believe (oh, and donate a small gift of $199.00). Sadly, all of this falls under the umbrella of Christianity. No wonder no one wants to accept Christianity. It too often feels like a bunch of people struggling with their own problems and pointing out other people's flaws. American Christianity has become a flipping side show.

The God-box induces fear. God is not big enough to handle diversity, individualism, culture, and even progress. That's why there becomes a greater push for a tightening of moral standards. I have heard among believers that we need a fire-and-brimstone revival. It's discouraging to me to hear that believers earnestly believe that the only way we can "win" others to Christ is to coerce people with fear and condemnation to conform to a holy God. Why can't we focus on His attributes of both love *and* justice? Or focus on the fact—not the myth—that He offers a peace that surpasses any other peace offered in this world? Is He not greater than the fear of His wrath? He was the same God that came and dined with sinners. He is so much grander than intimidation. I would like to suggest that the kind of revival we need is not one of fire but one of love.

You have not come to a mountain that can be touched and that is burning with fire; to darkness, gloom and storm; to a trumpet blast or to such a voice speaking words that those who heard it begged that no further word be spoken to them, because they could not bear what was commanded: "If even an animal touches the mountain, it must be stoned to death." The sight was so terrifying that Moses said, "I am trembling with fear." But you have come to Mount Zion, to the city of the living God, the heavenly Jerusalem. You have come to thousands upon thousands of angels in joyful assembly, to the church of the firstborn, whose names are written in heaven. You have come to God, the Judge of all, to the spirits of the righteous made perfect, to Jesus the mediator of a new covenant, and to the sprinkled blood that speaks a better word than the blood of Abel. Therefore, since we are receiving a kingdom that cannot be shaken, let us be thankful, and so worship God acceptably with reverence and awe, for our "God is a consuming fire." (Hebrews 12:18–24, 28–29)

We need a revival in which the broken, sick and vile have a home in the arms of Christ—where superficial moral behavior is no longer the litmus test of a good Christian. We need the modern day Pharisaical formulas to take a back seat to the power of a personal prayer life filled with confession, raw emotion, and intimacy. I have heard it said by a wise pastor that we have a "Jesus Plus" gospel, and I couldn't agree more. If only we could strip away the "plus" and focus on the truth of the gospel. God is a holy God who, without Christ's atonement, could not commune with sinners.

Therefore, brothers and sisters, since we have confidence to enter the Most Holy Place by the blood of Jesus, by a new and living way opened for us through the curtain, that is, his body, and since we have a great priest over the house of God, let us draw near to God with a sincere heart and with the full assurance that faith brings, having our hearts sprinkled to cleanse us from a guilty conscience and having our bodies washed with pure water. Let us hold unswervingly to the hope we profess, for he who promised is faithful. And let us consider how we may spur one another on toward love and good deeds, not giving up meeting together, as some are in the habit of doing, but encouraging one another— and all the more as you see the Day approaching...Since we have been justified through faith, we have peace with God through our Lord Jesus Christ, through whom we have gained access by faith into this grace in which we now stand. (Hebrews 10:19–25, Romans 5:1–2)

That's the gospel in which we need to place our energy. The fact that Jesus has absorbed the wrath of the awe-consuming holy God so that we can come boldly, reverently, and purely to His throne is the beauty of it all. Let's have a revival about that!

We need to remove the weight of "righteous living" and first and foremost focus on the fundamentals. But that scares people. They fear that if you remove the significance of "righteous living," America will literally go to hell in a handbasket. But it's all backwards. The church is preaching, "Jesus loves the 'in-casts'. The outcasts will remain 'out' until they begin cleaning up their lives." Although the God-box followers won't admit it, it's easier to control a morally good life. There are rules to follow, ways to behave, and lines not to cross. Everything has its place and the way it should be. There is a lack of trust and a whole lot of fear in this way of living out one's faith. A free-flowing, spirit-driven life is much harder to control. There's more gray and less black and white. It is unmanageable by outsiders, unstoppable by observers, and could even have the risk of looking counterintuitive to the God-box religion. It can be messy and unpredictable, but it will always be a God-ordained adventure with a God-ordained sense of order (not a religious-ordained sense of order).

I have heard of children going off to college and going through a period of searching and questioning. Their families are filled with much angst and worry that their child will leave God. I can understand this parental concern, but it's important to remember that God is capable of handling doubt. That child has not left His hand. He is a God who continues to woo His children back to Himself, over and over again like a relentless lover. And if that child chooses to leave God, well, that faith was never genuine to begin with. God will always keep His end of the covenant. He won't let His true child slip out of His hands.

I must caution that in no way am I stating that God does not have a deep passion for righteous living. He does, very much so. 1 Peter 1:14–19 commands His people,

> As obedient children, do not conform to the evil desires you had when you lived in ignorance. But just as he who called you is holy, so be holy in all you do; for it is written: "Be holy, because I am holy." Since you call on a Father who judges each person's

work impartially, live out your time as foreigners here in reverent fear. For you know that it was not with perishable things such as silver or gold that you were redeemed from the empty way of life handed down to you from your ancestors, but with the precious blood of Christ, a lamb without blemish or defect.

A couple things...first, this idea of holiness is something that God desires for the whole world (Christians and non-Christians alike), but the mandate is for Christians. Why do we expect people who do not claim to believe in this God of the Bible to act like Christians do? Secondly, being holy is a huge mandate, but that's why believers are given the Holy Spirit. This is a task impossible to carry out in our own God-box world. Those who live in the God-box rely on moral constructs of the religion to carry out the holiness. Holiness has much to do with faith, much to do with living in the Spirit and resting in His working. The Spirit works from the inside out, the God-box works from the outside in. We were bought with a price, Christ's blood; why, then, do we minimize our religion to a list of moral standards? Why don't we maximize it to a life of abiding faith and trust from which moral fruit will result? Righteous lifestyles and living are a mandate, but apparent "righteous lifestyles and living" that stem from fear-induced religiosity hidden by a façade of correct behavior is a far cry from living a life in the Spirit, who "will guide you into all the truth" (John 16:12–15). It is intimacy—not religiosity—that yields transformation.

Sadly, other religions appear to offer more peace, more acceptance, more love, and more personal transformation than Christianity. There is a strong affinity for mysticism but not for

Jesus. There is a strong yearning for inner peace but a rejection of the church. There is a strong craving for intellectual challenge but a hesitation to claim that the Bible is credible. The fact is that true Christianity, the true Good News, is available to all and offers more validity, more purpose, and more hope for transformation than any other competing religion. It's all right there at our fingertips, all within reach, but there has been such an abuse and misuse of the gospel that it has become unrecognizable.

I am convinced that God is big enough to handle our humanity. I believe He can handle our questions, even the hard ones, at those times when we get close to not believing in Him. I believe that He is a gentleman, offering Himself with the risk of rejection. I believe that His primary goal is for us to know Him relationally and intimately, and out of that flows fruit. And I believe all this because I've lived through years of intense doubting, deliberating, and searching only to find that the truth lies in Him. He is not an angry wizard who reacts capriciously to humankind's offenses. He doesn't give up on us no matter how much we give up on Him. He is a God who is real, alive, moving, and interested in our personal lives.

God can't be "summed up," nor is He a mystery to be solved. The Almighty is not a formula that can be learned to yield a constant result. In Him is a depth and a love so profound and unfathomable that truly exploring with Him will leave you far from bored. He is a lover that longs to be known. People are scared to talk to God, but being afraid of Him is keeping you from the most enjoyable adventure of your life. I understand people who don't like the church thing—too often the experience doesn't match with the God of the Bible. And I'm not encouraging people to forsake the church community, because a lot of good can come from being with a group of others who follow the living God (Hebrews 10:25). This institution was God's idea for our own good. You need others, and the more you grow in your faith, the more you will begin to realize you need the support and fellowship of other believers. Being a Christian is not for the faint of heart.

If someone wanted to "find" God, my first response would not be to tell them to practice good morals, to stop sinning, or even to read the Bible. My first advice would be to stop worrying about how good or bad you are and to start praying. But not just the Hail Mary or the Lord's Prayer—not just the impersonal prayers that you offer up because you must, or the ones you said when you were a kid because your mom or dad made you. I'm saying talk to Him as you would talk to your best friend. Be real! Be honest! Be personal. If that means telling Him that you don't trust Him, then do it. If that means telling Him that you feel worthless, then do it. If that means asking Him why your son died from cancer, then do it. If that means telling Him you hate your life or don't like Him...then do it! He can handle it. Talk to Him. Ask Him questions. Tell Him exactly what you're feeling. He was human, He understands and He will answer. It may not be in the timing you want or come in the way you'd planned, but be open, expectant, and available. And be patient. Some prayers can take years to be answered. God's timetable is most assuredly not our own. He's not standing in Heaven holding a checklist and making tally marks under columns labeled "good deeds" and "bad deeds." Our tally marks are not the things that save us. He's standing there, arms wide open, offering forgiveness, ready to embrace you no matter your past or present condition. He just wants a relationship with you, and He longs, more than anything, to be desired by you more than your next breath. The rest of the stuff will fall into place. If you need to quit smoking, you can get there. If you need to find purpose, you can find it. If you need to stop an addiction, you can overcome it. But don't focus on fixing those things on your own strength before you come near to God. First, come into His presence no matter your present condition, no matter your present sins or hang-ups. I mean, fully, truly, whole-heartedly journey with the living God and talk to Him intimately and honestly. That's when the real God enters raw emotion and reveals living proof of a transformed life to a thirsty world.

Chapter 8

Puke and Transformation

I am a tried-and-true germophobe. I often disinfect my cell phone, steering wheel, handles, and remotes. If, on the unfortunate occasion the dishwasher is not an option, I add bleach to my dish detergent to effectively wash the dishes. I always use nitrile gloves when dealing with raw meat. (Needless to say, the Thanksgiving Day turkey prep about did me in.) And, if given the opportunity, I would order a drink of Lysol with my dinner during flu season.

So what can I say? Is it such a crime to love disinfectants? My husband is the exact opposite. He believes germs are ubiquitous and that God gave us an immune system for a reason. (God truly does have a sense of humor!) But I remain steadfast in the belief that every nose blow, toilet flush, and grocery store visit deserve a thorough lather-and-suds handwashing experience to follow.

Oddly enough, I find myself working in the medical field. (My dad has often said I missed my calling as a health inspector.) Let's just say, I ain't your best friend, let-me-hold-your-hair-back type of gal when someone is about to throw up. I will leave you, abandon you, and oftentimes look at you like you have the black plague. I once made my mother wear a mask when she had the stomach flu. I disinfected things so "well" at her house that apparently the spray took the varnish off the dining room table and chairs. She banned me from using anything other than soap on the furniture after that.

I always let anybody I'm close to or going to be around for an extended period of time know that I will not help them if they are throwing up. If they have a cold, we can be friends; if they are puking or gagging…the friendship is temporarily over until certain microbes are permanently destroyed. My roommate in college woke me up one morning around five a.m. She tapped me on the shoulder and quietly whispered, "Rebecca, I think I'm going to be sick, so you might want to leave." I tell you, I never felt so awake that early in the morning. I moved out of our room for an entire week and crashed on a couch in my other friends' dorm. So, I guess I suffer from a severe case of emetophobia (or so they call it), and I will go to great lengths to avoid any situation in which I will have to confront it. Ah, I can feel my stomach churning just from writing about this!

Fear, especially stupid, irrational fear, is crippling. It causes you to do weird things, and it usually isn't isolated. One fear can lead to another—the original fear is the base of many others. Fear quickly controls you, which in turn causes you to control other things in your life so that you don't have to face them. Fear and control hold hands and become partners. They can become so united that they squeeze you—the true you—out. Once they butt the true you out (the person you were meant to be), they leave only enough room for the false you to come out...the one that operates from insecurity and manipulation. They are quite a domineering duo—they frequently aid in the destruction of many reputations or at least breed prime opportunities for embarrassment. I really do wish they would get a divorce.

It's quite obvious what this damaging duo can do to a single human being, but what if they could spread their likeness to groups or organizations? What would that look like? Some churches in America. Okay, okay, that might be a little harsh, but what if there is some truth to this concept? Are the churches we see today operating out of fear, or out of a lack of fear? To piggyback off of the previous chapter, have they lost their identity as a people set apart to show love, grace, justice, and expressions of a living, moving Spirit? Is it not possible that the destructive duo has butted out the true identity of the church?

A quick sweep across America's population undoubtedly proves that people have lost a sense of *fear* (as in holy awe and awareness of righteousness) and reverence for God or even any god, for that matter. And I can't deny that, yes, churches have catered to this by painting God as a jolly teddy bear. So although this is a valid point worth exploring, I find another matter even closer to my heart.

If God created the intricacy of an atom in tandem with a universe that expands light-years in shape and has provided eons of wonder...if God, who has masterfully stepped out of time yet still is able to commune with us in our finite minds...if this God who is able to know billions of people intimately and know the number of hairs on each of their heads, or how many grains of sand have ever existed...if this God is really who He says He is, then why are our churches so dead, so scared...so powerless? As American Christians, if we worship this God, then how can the rest of America look upon us with disgust, rejection, and even hatred? Should they not be so moved and so intrigued that they can't help but want to know more? Of course, we could always blame this problem on the depravity of man and the wickedness of hearts—that's not entirely false. However, those things aren't entirely to blame. And yes, it's true that even in Jesus' time, people hated Christians. Jesus warns his disciples that this hatred is a part of the cost of following him. But maybe it's also true that churches have lost their identity. Maybe they live a safe, fear-ridden life as a community instead of living by the Spirit, who is as unpredictable as the wind. Maybe the church has traded in the power that raised Christ from the dead for misperceived security and subtle complacency. Maybe fear of death, fear of persecution, fear of decreasing "numbers," fear of losing money, fear of being rejected by society, fear of looking too conservative or too liberal, fear of offending others, fear of having their plans thwarted, fear of not being able to build the bigger and better building, fear of getting stained by the sinners, fear of getting their good name smudged by inner-city problems, fear of losing a member to another church, fear of people backsliding, fear of not being able to control how the congregation conducts themselves, fear of the cookie-cutter Christian life looking like a misshapen pile of dough…fear, fear, fear….yes, maybe, I'm afraid that fear has caused many American Churches to begin to lose their way.

I can't blame people who don't know Christ for not having any respect for Him. Christians can't even get along with each other, so why would they think the "leader" of the group was any different? To be honest, sometimes I don't even like *us*. When we disagree, we split off and form a new denomination. I had a teacher tell me once that there are thirty thousand denominations in America. Thirty thousand! Let's say that this professor is off, that somehow, he got a bad batch of stats. Even still, I can go down a list of denominations just in my own small town. I don't think it was meant to be this way. I don't think that Jesus, when he put Peter in charge of the churches, commanded him by saying, "Now go and make thousands of denominations with thousands of people pitted against each other and disassociated with one another." I mean, that could be in Third Corinthians or something, but I haven't read it. Christ said, "By this all men will know that you are my disciples, if you love one another" (John 13:35). And under the umbrella of love falls attributes of patience, kindness, protection, trust, and forbearance.

> Love is patient, love is kind. It does not envy, it does not boast, it is not proud. It does not dishonor others, it is not self-seeking, it is not easily angered, it keeps no record of wrongs. Love does not delight in evil but rejoices with the truth. It always protects, always trusts, always hopes, always perseveres. (1 Cor. 13:4–7)

This is hard stuff, not just sweet thoughts often read at a wedding.

Does the church really see the damage we're doing in our efforts to try to do the "right" thing? At what cost? When does the "right" thing actually become wrong? I have a friend who shared with me the story about the time she first brought her boyfriend to her church. She was excited for him to come but nervous because she was afraid that he might be "cornered." Her fears came true. After the service, during mingling time, she was introducing him to people. And sure enough, another young gentleman, who was around the same age, asked her boyfriend, "If you were to die today, why should God let you into His Kingdom?" The young man proceeded to go through the Ten Commandments, asking her boyfriend if he'd ever broken any of these. Although the tension between the two men was noticeable, the young man persisted in sharing the gospel, and the conversation dragged on until mingling time was nearly over. Needless to say, the boyfriend never returned to that church, and my friend, well, she felt really embarrassed. She wasn't embarrassed about the gospel being shared: She was embarrassed by the tact that was used to share it. The gospel is synonymous with "good news." Good news comes as water to a parched soul; it's life giving. It shouldn't be shared as a formula, dry and stressful, like a calculus class. Yeah, sure, my friend's boyfriend heard the gospel, but at what cost? How much damage did it do? He didn't agree to be "cornered." He was forced. He wasn't asked if he felt like sharing his past sins with another sinner; he was pressured to respond. Yes, he "heard" the gospel, but did he actually hear it? No—what he actually heard was judgment, pressure, tension, accusations from a "loving" stranger. He heard loud, overbearing, obnoxious cymbals.

> If I speak in the tongues of men or of angels, but do not have love, I am only a resounding gong or a clanging cymbal. If I have the gift of prophecy and can fathom all mysteries and all knowledge, and if I have a faith that can move mountains, but do not have love, I am nothing. If I give all I possess to the poor and give over my body to hardship that I may boast, but do not have love, I gain nothing. (1 Cor 13:1-3)

So here we find ourselves in the twenty-first century, thousands of years from the ancient verse, doing many, many things for the sake of preserving the message of Christ while all the while forgetting that maybe the first part of preserving that message is meeting a person where they are, with the questions they have, the wounds they carry, the bitterness they bear, and the "unright," unwholesome, unhealthy lifestyles with which they're currently dealing. Did God get glory that day in the back-of-the-church chitchat? I don't know. Did the angels start to sing because another person was added to the body of believers? Well, I didn't hear them. Did a seed of truth get planted? Quite possibly—God can use anything. Or was God grieved? Maybe, just maybe he was watching and saying, "No, no, no...you forgot the love. You forgot the love! He isn't a project, he is my beloved. Tell him I love him. No, better yet, *show* him I love him. He needs to know."

But therein "lies the rub"; you can spend all day basking in love but forget the truth. Many churches have tried on the dogmas passed down from the original church fathers and have suddenly found themselves nitpicking the traditional and trying on some new beliefs for size. This is just as damaging, because many churches have given up the tried and tested original truths for a cheap and trendy alternative. Denominations have changed their stances on long-standing doctrines because they fear society's backlash. They have formulated God in their image so that Christianity's attire becomes more attractive, less scratchy, and a more popular style to don. These churches fear being labeled haters or bigots. They fear the pushback that occurs when they take a stand on controversy. They fear persecution and falsely rationalize that their actions are rooted in love rather than in peer pressure. It is possible for a church to "love" a person into hell if they are not careful.

If a patient goes to a doctor to find out why they are losing weight, feeling fatigued, and experiencing pain, and the doctor simply spends time making them feel better by giving them a pep talk, telling them what coffee to buy to keep them energized, and giving them compliments to change their perspective on how they feel about themselves, what good would that do? A person goes to a doctor to find out why they're sick and what their treatment options are. They want the doctor to tell them the truth. How would the patient benefit if the doctor were too afraid to offend them by giving them the true diagnosis of their condition? How is it loving to only make a person feel good at the expense of withholding the truth? We're humans—we're creatures that like to be liked, but at what cost?

Ephesians 4:15 instructs believers to speak the truth in love, and John 1:14 reminds us that Jesus came in the fullness of all grace and truth. This is the tension of the true identity of the church. It is a beacon that should model its leader—Jesus Christ—speaking and displaying all truth in both grace and love. Love should not be usurped by truth, as in the scenario of my friend's boyfriend, but neither should truth be usurped by love, as in the case of the sick patient.

I have heard it said (by someone I really respect and trust) that doctrine is everything. Truthfully, this soured in my soul like a bad onion. I would like to challenge that notion. I am not by any means trying to minimize the importance or necessity of sound doctrine. I'm rather arguing that good doctrine leads to great brain power and knowledge, but focusing only on doctrine can cause us to quickly circumvent the heart. It seems as if many churches have the mind but have lost the heart. Doctrine is not everything but is half of the whole. Sound doctrine is the fertile soil in which seeds of truth get planted. Soul-searching, solitude, and spiritual formation are the incubators in which the plants take root, get water, and ultimately bloom. Not every disagreement or biblical topic is a hill to die on. Satan has the body of Christ so distracted by disagreements that we're too busy attempting to cool the embers within the church and fail to see the raging fire surrounding us.

Society is shifting, and with this new era comes a changing approach to relevant outreach. People aren't going to church for a place of support, comfort, and healing because many churches have become a place of judgment and seem fake. These churches have lost their platform for exemplifying transformative differences because they themselves are not experiencing the transformation. When a church spends all its time on head knowledge or superficial fluff, its heart begins to shrivel. Just as you can't fuel a body by ingesting only water or a candy bar, so the church begins to waste away from a lack of soul-touching truths. You can maintain a church, you can keep a group of people attending, you can still be obedient and useful to God, but when you don't join knowledge with the spirit, the transformative potential remains dormant and less effective.

In this weakened state, the Church begins to operate out of its false self, losing its identity. Paul, in his letter to Timothy, said, "God did not give us a spirit of timidity, but a spirit of power, of love and of self-discipline" (2 Timothy 1:7). Paul explained how Christians were given a different spirit—one of power, love, and self-discipline. This is the spirit by which we, all of us individually, were designed to live by—the spirit of God—the Holy Spirit. If the church, which comprises multitudes of individuals, were operating with this very same spirit, then the church as a unit should exude power, love, and self-discipline, as well. This is our true identity individually and also as a part of the church. This identity is absent of timidity. Fear and control are antithesis of the true identity.

Bear with me. Although the following passage is long, it has some deep truths that get at what I'm trying to explain:

> Make every effort to live in peace with all men and to be holy; without holiness no one will see the Lord. See to it that no one misses the grace of God and that no bitter root grows up to cause trouble and defile many. See that no one is sexually immoral, or is godless like Esau, who for a single meal sold his inheritance rights as the oldest son. Afterward, as you know, when he wanted to inherit this blessing, he was rejected. He could bring about no change of mind, though he sought the blessing with tears. You have not come to a mountain that can be touched and that is burning with fire; to darkness, gloom and storm; to a trumpet blast or to such a voice speaking words that those who heard it begged that no further word be spoken to them, because they could not bear what was commanded: "If even an animal touches the mountain, it must be stoned." The sight was so terrifying that Moses said, "I am trembling with fear." But you have come to Mount

Zion, to the heavenly Jerusalem, the city of the living God. You have come to thousands upon thousands of angels in joyful assembly, to the church of the firstborn, whose names are written in heaven. You have come to God, the judge of all men, to the spirits of righteous men made perfect, to Jesus the mediator of a new covenant, and to the sprinkled blood that speaks a better word than the blood of Abel. See to it that you do not refuse him who speaks. If they did not escape when they refused him who warned them on earth, how much less will we, if we turn away from him who warns us from heaven? At that time his voice shook the earth, but now he has promised, "Once more I will shake not only the earth but also the heavens." The words "once more" indicate the removing of what can be shaken—that is, created things—so that what cannot be shaken may remain. Therefore, since we are receiving a kingdom that cannot be shaken, let us be thankful, and so worship God acceptably with reverence and awe, for our "God is a consuming fire." (Hebrews 12:14–29)

Basically, the author is charging the audience to listen. It's as if he's saying, "this God who we worship is the same One who was there when Esau traded in his inheritance for a simple bowl of soup, the same God who is so holy and pure that even Moses trembled at his majesty, the same God who is a righteous judge of all mankind, the same God who anointed Jesus to be a mediator and Lord of all lords, the same God who has the power to create or destroy the universe if it be His will...this God, this living God, still speaks. And when He speaks...listen. The things this God speaks of are eternal, transformative, and powerful—He speaks of the Kingdom He has given, which cannot be shaken, now or ever. This God is likened to a consuming fire. Because this God is so great, so just, so pure, so powerful...why do we hold on to bitterness? Why do we insist on arguing and dividing over every minor detail? Why do we act as if we have no self-control when this mighty God is the author and giver of it? Why don't we "seek peace and pursue it" (Psalm 34:14)? This author makes the point that we're not to live out of weakness and the fear that comes from control or distrust, but rather we're to live with the fear of the majesty of a mighty, infinite God who speaks and is deserving of our attention. He does not just want a token thought, or a fleeting moment. He wants to partner with us in restoring the world. He chooses us to get His message out, He chooses us to heal, He chooses us to share His love with others, He chooses us to be transformed and to transform others. If we serve this great of a God, then how can we experience Him and not be transformed?

The heart is the temple of our bodies. This is where the holy God comes to meet us. We can spend a whole life "knowing" God with our minds, learning about God but not allowing God into our temple. We may think we're experiencing Him, but because we're not being transformed, we are truly not experiencing Him. Experiencing God demands our vulnerability. That means we allow Him entry into our darkest places, our most shameful thoughts... the ugliest parts we have. Transformation does not happen unless we experience God in the wounds and lies we have carried with us. These are the places that doctrine can't reach and superficial words can't even mildly touch. Transformed lives are birthed out of formational prayer, in which these areas are safely exposed to the light of Christ.

The song, "New Morning" by Alpha Rev inspires me every time I hear it. (Now, I know that some are probably going to be offended by the lyrics, but just look past the one word of uneasiness and try to catch the message.)

I don't give a damn about the castle on the hill
all the gold that we could eat, or the horse you had for sale
No, I'm getting kinda rich on the side of any soul alive

I don't give a damn if I'm running from the law
when my money's not enough and they come and take it all
No, I'm getting kinda rich on the side of any soul alive

Have you heard the Mona Lisa?
Have you heard who you are?
You're a new morning
You're a new morning

Wanna be ok when I'm sitting here alone
Not just thinking of the ways that I could have done it wrong
No, I'm getting kinda rich on the side of any soul alive
Have you heard the Mona Lisa?
Have you heard who you are?
You're a new morning
You're a new morning
You're a new morning
Now, you're a new morning now[7]

This is simply beautiful. The song touches something deep within me. What's more enriching than a soul coming alive to whom they were meant to be? Money and possessions can't even begin to compete with the inspiring allure of a person truly living. The artists acknowledge that after such splendor, why waste time on guilt and on pondering all the ways you aren't *enough*? No, there is so much more. Think about it—the weight of glory we bear when we live out the image of an almighty God is beyond the historical masterpiece of a Mona Lisa. I love how they say in the song, "have you heard the Mona Lisa?" It's ironic. Have you heard it? A soul alive surpasses just being "seen"—no, a soul alive is *heard*. It speaks. You're a new morning...a dawn of possibilities, depth, beauty, redemption...there is no limit on how God can use you, unless you choose to limit Him.

So much of how we live our lives is based on what we believe in the core of who we are. If you believe that you're worthless, you live as if you are of no value and deserve the bad things that happen to you. If you believe that you're a burden, then you live as though you're always in the way or always a problem for others to deal with. If you have little confidence, you act less assured and begin to render yourself useless to accomplish bigger tasks. If you believe that you're dirty, you live as if it's okay to be treated with disrespect and degradation. What we believe about ourselves affects how we live. So we can work on these qualities. We can strive to do better. We can follow all the rules. We can quit smoking, stop swearing, hold our temper, spend less money...etc. We can do all these noble things by using our own effort, but we're only painting over the water cracks on the ceiling and trying to hide the foundational damage, when the truth is, we need to tear the cracked part out and replace the bad with the good piece of drywall. So it is with our hearts. We can mightily work to change ourselves for the better (e.g., make New Year's resolutions) and fail because we keep painting over the crack in the ceiling and wonder why it's still leaking. Paint all you want, but the ceiling will still leak until that crack gets patched.

Our churches lack formational prayers and spiritual change. We are in dire need of living not only in truth but in spirit. I can't help but wonder if souls are parched simply because they lack time or assistance in examining the autonomy of their souls in the light of Christ. It may be possible that people are trying to become "filled by the spirit" from the "outside in" instead of from the "inside out." They may be trying to heal their wounds by applying more Band-Aids instead of ingesting the antibiotic. Humans walk around like wounded soldiers. We carry battle scars and deep, unresolved issues that take time to unpack, energy to hash out, and a desperate need to expose them to the light of Christ so that healing can begin and wholeness will unfold. People lack a safe place where personal issues, deep, raw emotions, and struggles can be exposed, challenged, and healed by the living God. We stay superficial in a sense, but to really grow, we need to delve into the reason behind the feeling, the question behind the question, and the fear behind the action. We need to go deep, not only doctrinally deep, but also spiritually and prayerfully deep in order to be transformed. There is a spirit of deadness, of dryness, and God is calling all of us to come alive now, not in the Kingdom in the afterlife, but in the Kingdom that has already come and is not fully here. Life is short, yet life is eternal.

And what God begins within our souls bridges into completion in Heaven. God has placed on each of us a passion, a desire—something we were created to do—to bring Him glory and even to bring us joy. I believe that it's God's desire to bring healing, freedom, and wholeness now. I believe that in order to receive those gifts He offers, we must be intentional about it. It may take a sacrifice of time or vulnerability. It may feel risky because it steps out of the confines of doctrine and into the uniqueness of the Spirit's moving (John 3:8), and the Spirit's moving cannot be controlled, it can only be surrendered to.

An environment sensitive to the Spirit should be an environment free from judgment. A safe place is wherever people can face both themselves and God in complete honesty about who they are. And in the safe place, God will meet them and accept them. It is not a place where a person is told what they "should" do or what they are "not doing enough of." It's a time to recognize and become aware of all they are (both good and bad) and all that God is. It's the very place where the two connect. It should be an environment that is life-giving and only encourages the believer to become more of who they were always meant to be, not a place to kick them when they're down. Spiritual formation is essential for living a healthy and intentional life for God. It's what enables us to be transformed and live out the good works God has prepared for each of us to do (Eph 2:10). When we are truly filled with the Spirit and listening to His personal and individual leading of our hearts, then we can really live out, personally and corporately, Christ to others. This is when the true identity of the church is restored, because we begin to live out of the power, love, and self-discipline that has already been vested to us.

During my vacation in Florida, I remember floating atop of the calm ocean waves. It was peaceful to be supported by the warm water and to feel the balmy breezes as the sun's rays enveloped me. Absolutely serene! In order to float I had to trust the water, relax, and yield to the motion of the wave. As I trusted the current, I was aware that a big wave could come along and flip me. I could also drift far from shore or get caught by an undertow. Although it was so peaceful, it was also very unpredictable. Following the Spirit's working in your heart is kind of like that. You ride the waves, but you're never out of sight of the Son. It is when you are on the wave that you must be most at peace, so you can float above the muck and avoid the sharp shells on the ocean's bottom. Safer are you when you are carried by the wave than when you fight against its power.

Chapter 9

Leading

One time, several years ago, I was sitting down to eat lunch when I turned on the TV and began flipping through the channels. I paused on a channel featuring televangelist Benny Hinn's *This is Your Day* broadcast. With my finger still on the TV remote and the other hand reaching for my lunch, my eyes remained glued to the TV, more out of curiosity than interest, like watching a bad car accident. He was talking about financial anointing and selecting random passages from the Old Testament to support his claim. He requested financial support from the audience (mind you, this was no small audience but thousands of spectators, both in person and via the TV) in exchange for anointing powers and blessings from God. Unlike other "health and wealth prosperity gospels," he purported that God would financially bless people with monetary and material abundance because of their donations to his ministry. At the end of the episode was an extra plea for monetary contributions, like an infomercial that says, "but wait there's more, a limited time offer." There was an extremely expensive Bible with multicolored ink that was advertised to promise healing effects because of its special font. The lure was that purchasing and reading this "special" Bible would bring physical healing. After this episode, I went to the computer and sent a poignant email message to Benny Hinn Ministries, expressing to them my vexation. Thousands of people were trusting wolves in sheep's clothing, giving money to receive blessings or healing, and all of this was being done in the name of Jesus. It was sickening.

The abuse and misuse of a belief leads to skepticism and to a lack of credibility. We see this all the time in our society. News headings read, "Woman finds image of Jesus in her waffle, affirming her decision to leave her husband," or "Man lives in minivan after God tells him not to work." Right and left, people claim they "hear" from God, but do their actions really resemble the picture of Jesus portrayed in Scripture? These types of disconnects make you either doubt God's character or, more often, doubt that people are really being "led by God."

Remember in elementary school, how you were never allowed to chew gum? It was against the rules. Why couldn't we enjoy the succulent taste of Double Bubble after recess? Because somebody ruined it for us. Kids proved themselves untrustworthy. Instead of discarding the gum in the trash, the slobbery ball of cohesive goodness would be stuck under chairs, spit on the ground, and left as a surprise on the underbelly of the desk. The same is true with claims about hearing from God. So many people have improperly used this excuse as a means to carry out their own sin-bent, flawed-perception, self-centered agendas. But just as the children misusing chewing gum, should one bad apple ruin it for all? Isn't it possible that some could properly handle the privilege even though others may not?

I guess what I'm encouraging, here, is the idea conveyed in an old adage: "Don't throw the baby out with the bath water." I remember talking with my now-husband, Chris, at the beginning of our dating days. In our conversations, I would share with him what I felt God was doing in my life and where He was leading me. I would use phrases like, "I feel like God is telling me," "I know God is teaching me," and "I feel like He is saying..." Chris would sometimes reply with a disheartening reprimand: "Keep your feet on the ground; your head is in the clouds," "This is a red flag," or "Stop trying to decide what God is trying to do in your life." I remember I would feel very misunderstood, but I guess there was some truth in the mix of it all. What Chris was cautioning me against was emotional radicalism.

Some people get so wrapped up in their emotions that what they "feel" is what they deem to be true. Although, I don't believe I misused the claims of God's leading, I can understand Chris' reservations, and it's wise for me to pause and check my heart. Some Christians who have grown up in a church or in Christian homes will equate church authority or parental authority with the voice of God. This can be misleading and damaging. Some churches are more charismatic, and so the only way to know the Holy Spirit is leading is by a heightened sense of emotion. Again, this can be confusing.

So, what can we concretely deduce from what Scripture provides? I think it's evident, just by a quick review of text found in the Bible, that first, we know that there is a Creator God. This Creator made humans (we don't need to debate how—evolution, the Big Bang, creationism, etc. All we need to agree on is that in some fashion He created the existence in which we find ourselves). Then, we have 66 books in which the Creator God speaks to humans. Sometimes this is audible (the first five books of the Bible), sometimes He speaks through a messenger, such as a prophet (Isaiah, Jeremiah, Habakkuk, etc.), sometimes through Jesus (Matthew, Mark, Luke, John, etc.), and sometimes through the Holy Spirit (the Epistles and the Book of Acts). Whether or not you agree with the frequency, the method, or the details of how God speaks, what can be deduced from a quick survey of Scripture is that the Bible portrays a God that does in fact speak to humans. Can we agree on this point?

Assuming you said yes to the above question, I would like to expound further. Why would God speak to His creation if He did not care about them? I don't spend much time conversing with people that I don't know. I don't call up a stranger and tell them about my dreams and hopes for the future. I don't tell the guy in the grocery store sweet affections. I don't mean to sound callous, but frankly, I don't care, and neither do they. I don't have love for them. Yes, I have love, in general, for mankind as a whole, but I don't have a relationship with these people. There is really nothing for me to talk to them about, nothing really to share. All the private information in my life is doled out carefully to those I care about and who also care about me. And that's what we see with God. God doesn't treat mankind like strangers or like the guy in the grocery store—He treats them like family. He has something to say to them because He does care.

When I speak of hearing God's "voice" or God "speaking," I'm not referring to an audible voice; however, I'm not in a position to deny that God still does speak audibly. He did in the Old Testament, so can He now? I suppose. However, my personal theological stance is that God used direct, audible verbalization of His will in the Old Testament. He used more signs and wonders and physical manifestations to communicate His direction because the time predated Jesus and the Holy Spirit. To sum it up, I believe that God's voice was more audible and that He overtly and directly intervened in the Old Testament. Once on Earth, Jesus was the full radiance and resemblance of God, so what He did was to display God's voice in action. God's voice was manifest through Jesus. Once Jesus left, he tells us in John 14:15–31 (among many other passages) that He will give us a direct counselor who will allow us to hear the voice of God within us, not so much audibly, but by a nudging, by a revelation of truth, by resonating Scripture, by peace or lack of peace, and by wisdom. This is the voice of God that we hear—the internal presence of the Holy Spirit imparted to believers, residing in them, and conveying God's truth. The Holy Spirit's job is to always point us back to Christ, and Christ's job was always to point us back to God the Father. To put it simply, when I speak of the "voice" of God, I am speaking mainly of the Holy Spirit illuminating truth about the personhood and sovereign will of God.

What I have found is that God is frequently speaking, but there are many times that we are not listening. We muck up the message with old wounds, insecurities, doubts, apathy, and disbelief, but God often has something to say. So how do you know if the Holy Spirit is leading? There are four ways to help you discern:

The voice of God is a still, soft voice.

The voice of God is life-giving.

The voice is glorifying to God.

The voice is consistent with Scripture.

There's a story in 1 Kings 19:11-13, that describes God as He is getting ready to appear to Elijah the prophet:

> The Lord said, "Go out and stand on the mountain in the presence of the Lord, for the Lord is about to pass by." Then a great and powerful wind tore the mountains apart and shattered the rocks before the Lord, but the Lord was not in the wind. After the wind there was an earthquake, but the Lord was not in the earthquake. After the earthquake came a fire, but the Lord was not in the fire. And after the fire came a gentle whisper. When Elijah heard it, he pulled his cloak over his face and went out and stood at the mouth of the cave."

Remember the lowly manger birth of Jesus? He wasn't born with pomp and circumstance. Remember the type of king that Jesus was? He didn't slaughter all the Romans or conquer a bunch of territory. Remember the humble beginnings of Joseph? He was in prison for many years before he was raised to a position of power and authority in Egypt. Is it not the nature of God to forgo glamour and prestige and to rather come in a gentle whisper? You know God is speaking to you when He is subtly nudging you to do something that builds His Kingdom. Does your sense of His leading increase your faith in God's abilities and not your own? Does it make you trust God deeper? Does it make you have compassion? Extend forgiveness? Take a step away from selfishness? Then you know that it is God's voice. When God speaks, He speaks into His cosmic plan. He doesn't speak into private, self-preserving, egocentric, corrupt, personal MO's. Instead He speaks to bring you and others into a closer dependence on Him.

Secondly, we know it's the voice of God when the voice is life-giving. Jesus tells us in John 10:10, "The thief comes only to steal and kill and destroy; I have come that they may have life, and have it to the full." Sin leads to death. A lack of sin leads to life. Jesus was about reversing the sin and death in this world. He wants to bring life—vitality, fullness, wholeness, peace, and reconciliation. Jesus does not want righteousness just so we can be perfect little beings, doing perfect little things. No, Jesus wants righteousness because it's best for us. It's what's healthiest. It's the best version of you that could possibly exist. And this brings pleasure to the Father.

If you are starting to feel guilty about something, you must first ask—did I truly do something wrong? Did I go against a moral standard that is in Scripture? Did I offend God? Half the time we feel guilty for failing to live up to the standards imposed on us by other people. I feel guilty because I didn't go to the family reunion. I feel guilty because I said "no" when my boss asked me to work overtime. Let me be clear. It's okay, and actually very healthy, to have autonomy. It's a very good thing to know your boundaries and limitations, and sometimes it's very necessary to say "no." Your "no" to another person's demand can be a "yes" to God. The voice of God will not be one of false guilt. It will not be guilt that says you did something wrong because you failed to meet expectations. It will not be guilt that shames you and strikes at the worth of who you are. These messages are from the thief that has come to kill and destroy. True guilt is life-giving. It provides a better option. It offers freedom from misery and death. It inspires you to be more instead of making you feel as though you are not enough. It will not kick you when you are down but rather will energize you to chase after wholeness.

The voice of God will always bring glory to Him. I remember being on the verge of making a life-altering decision. I realized that one option kept me close-minded and comfortable. The other option would be more of a risk, but it would lead to taking a step of faith. It opened up my mind to a bigger picture of God. I knew then that the second option was the voice of God leading me. Why? Because His name was being glorified, my understanding of His nature was being increased, and it beckoned something selfless and bigger than me, faith. What does it mean for God to be glorified? It means that His essence, His weightiness, His grandeur is entering the scenario. When the righteousness of God and the purity of His love is revealed—God is being glorified. When His sovereign hand is guiding the situation and control is being released to His power, God is being glorified. Look at the life of Jesus. In John 14:6–10, Jesus is talking with His disciples about the union formed by Him and the Father:

> Jesus answered, "I am the way and the truth and the life. No one comes to the Father except through me. If you really know me, you will know my Father as well. From now on, you do know him and have seen him." Philip said, "Lord, show us the Father and that will be enough for us." Jesus answered: "Don't you know me, Philip, even after I have been among you such a long time? Anyone who has seen me has seen the Father. How can you say, 'Show us the Father'? Don't you believe that I am in the Father, and that the Father is in me? The words I say to you I do not speak on my own

authority. Rather, it is the Father, living in me, who is doing his work."

Jesus was the very fulfillment of the glory of God. When we watch Jesus, we see that there is a keen interdependence with God the Father. He would go alone and pray to the Father. He would talk with the Father, even asking Him to remove the suffering He was about to endure on the cross, but submitting to His direction. Jesus would show compassion, be fearless, die to Himself, and die for others. The life of Christ was always in tune with the voice of the Father. When you start wondering if God is speaking to you, start asking yourself if what you're feeling called to do looks similar to the life of Christ.

When God speaks, His voice is heard through the Holy Spirit—God's Spirit within you. 1 Corinthians 2: 10–12 says,

> The Spirit searches all things, even the deep things of God. For who knows a person's thoughts except their own spirit within them? In the same way no one knows the thoughts of God except the Spirit of God. What we have received is not the spirit of the world, but the Spirit who is from God, so that we may understand what God has freely given us.

The Holy Spirit will not contradict Scripture because that would be equivalent to God contradicting Himself. Scripture was God's idea and God's composition. It is God's revelation of Himself so that man can see the story of the Divine played out over years. God takes great delight in unveiling His character through Scripture. Hebrews 4:12 affirms this. "For the word of God is alive and active. Sharper than any double-edged sword, it penetrates even to dividing soul and spirit, joints and marrow; it judges the thoughts and attitudes of the heart." The voice of God is most commonly heard through Scripture. When you read a passage and feel that slight twinge in your heart, you know that it's the voice of God. When you read a passage you've read a thousand times before, but suddenly it has a different meaning, that is the voice of God speaking. When you see a verse in passing, hear a verse read in a sermon, or connect with a character from the Bible, that's the voice of God. Can God speak outside of Scripture—yes! In fact, I believe He does so all the time. He will use friends, counsel from others, circumstances, music…etc. Heck, I believe He's used some ungodly things in life to convey truth about Himself. God is not confined by stuff found only at church. God is greater than all and uses all things to point a lost soul back to Him. But God has given us the gift of Scripture as a way to check these voices. If the impression or leading that you sense you are hearing is actually from God, it will align with the truth found in the Bible. It will be life-giving, it will be glorifying to God, and it will be a patient, constant, still, soft, nudging voice.

The beauty of God's voice is that it prevents us from being clones, encourages individuality, and embraces freedom—release from the sins and pleasures that cause death and pain. Jesus said in John 3:8, "The wind blows wherever it pleases. You hear its sound, but you cannot tell where it comes from or where it is going. So it is with everyone born of the Spirit." What God may be convicting me about at a particular time in my life, He may not be convicting you about, and vice versa. Just as God gives us manna for the day, He gives us only a portion of conviction for the day, otherwise we would be overwhelmed. Conviction would turn into heavy weights and defeat. God wants victory in our lives, and so He prunes us with one conviction at a time. The same goes with calling. Calling is a life-giving burden—an undeniable nudge from the Spirit. A person who feels called can't escape it because the nagging labor of love will not leave until the task is complete. Each person has been given a different calling in proportion to their God-given ability. Just as the wind blows wherever it pleases, so does the Holy Spirit's calling and conviction. Each of us holds different desires, special uniqueness, and diverse skills, and that's just the way God designed it. Together we work as one unit to accomplish His Kingdom goals—to love your neighbor as yourself. To love the Lord your God will all your heart, soul, and mind. To live courageously and righteously. To know God more deeply and help others to do the same. To reach out to the lost so that they finally have a heavenly home. To serve, submit, and enjoy the presence of His goodness.

Our job is to be open and sensitive to the voice of God. God is not a micromanager. He doesn't need to tell you what color socks to wear or whether or not you should take a shower at night or in the morning. He's given you the gift of wisdom and a sound mind so that you can reason through these trivial tasks. But what about the bigger things in life—marriage, changing jobs, what college to go to, how many kids to have, when to have kids, what house, where to move, retirement...etc. What about these things? Does God always have something to say? No, not always; sometimes He says yes, and sometimes He says no. God has set up moral standards. These, again, are outlined in Scripture. When you abide by these moral standards, you know you are within the moral will of God. God may not necessarily voice His direction when choosing between two moral options because both are good in His eyes. If the decision you make is life-giving, God glorifying, and consistent with the principles outlined in the Bible, then God deems it good for you. There are times where God may be speaking to you on a matter—often providing direction in a decision, conviction in an area of sin, or encouragement in areas of defeat. How do you know He's speaking? Again, by His still, soft nudging, the life-giving nature of the nudge, the God-glorifying possibilities of the journey, and the confirmation from Scripture. God is sovereign; He is the author of free will. Use your free will. Live, take risks, enjoy the challenges, explore uncharted territory, and love Him. God is for you, not against you. He speaks because He loves. Turn your ear to what He has to say. You might be pleasantly surprised.

Chapter 10

A Scholarly Attempt to Explain Pleasing

I think people, for the most part, long to do "good." I think they want to do something meaningful with their lives, something that makes a difference in the world. Many desire to add to the "rightness" of society. Now of course, there are always outliers—people who just want to earn money, people who don't care who they walk over as long as they put fame in their name. There are always people who operate on self-serving platforms and put very little time into thinking about others. But my mind questions if maybe they, too, when they were in their formative years, had that same desire to do good. Maybe they tried and received the message that they failed. Or maybe they were told that their good was still not good enough, and in their defeat, they gave up and did what felt right.

A frequent nagging whisper that I "just can't get it right" has often surfaced in my conscience. Try as I might, I still wasn't good enough. This belief seemed to be solidified when studying the Old Testament God. I'd heard about forgiveness, learned about grace and salvation at a very early age, yet I never felt relief from my minor and major screw-ups. This carried into my adult years, but along with the belief came more outward symptoms of a heart striving with God. I would get angry quickly and turn to self-loathing regularly. I was a disappointment to myself—how could I not be a disappointment to God?

I would often read in the New Testament about this concept of "pleasing" God. I hated that word. I regularly condemned myself because I knew that I fell short of pleasing God on a very consistent basis. I wasn't compassionate enough, I wasn't selfless enough, I wasn't pure enough, I was too angry, I was too mouthy, I was too much and not enough—I was a failure. Although I knew Jesus had forgiven me and saved me, I would reason within myself that yes, I had been forgiven, but sadly, I was still a giant disappointment to a holy God. I would then hate myself for it, feeling unworthy. I knew that hating myself was a sin, but yet, it felt so natural and right—it was penance, a response that seemed warranted. This cyclical battle was so frequent for so many years that defeat felt more like a home than a prison. I began to accept that this was all part of the good news of Jesus. Yes, we are forgiven, but God is still not happy with us. It's not the dream ending I wanted, but life isn't about dream endings—I should just be grateful that I wasn't going to spend an eternity in hell.

I was asked to speak at a Woman's Conference on Romans chapter 8. In verse 8, the loaded word "please" butted its ugly head again. How was I supposed to explain this, when, for years, this had been a point of angst in my personal life? I knew I would need to do some research, get into the Greek, and delve into the scholarly wisdom passed down by theologians in years past. So, like I always do when I'm in a quandary with my faith, I put my feet to the ground and my nose to the books.

I researched the doctrine of impassivity and impassibility. Impassivity and impassibility are attributes ascribed to God, in which God does not feel. He does not mourn or grieve. He does not feel exhilarated or excited. He is unmoved, unemotional. Now some sides of the camp state that God does not feel at all—that He's completely straight-faced. Other sides of the camp, however, would venture to say that God does indeed feel but does not become overwhelmed by His feelings, as humans do. He would not be grieved to the point of feeling loss or less than Himself—His fullness and essence are unaffected. Now as I researched this—in the deepest part of me—I was hoping that this doctrine of impassivity would be key. I was hoping that it would eradicate my belief that God actually "felt" one way or another toward me when I sinned or even when I was victorious against sin. I was okay forfeiting the idea that God may not rejoice over my good deeds as long as I knew He wasn't unhappy with me when I committed sin. What I wanted was a God who did not feel, because that meant I couldn't hurt this God.

After doing more research on the doctrine of impassibility, I was still not convinced that God did not feel. I was making progress in accepting this doctrine, but something was still not answered. I ran across Ephesians 4:29–30,

> Let no corrupt talk come out of your mouths, but only such as is good for building up, as fits the occasion, that it may give grace to those who hear. And do not grieve the Holy Spirit of God, by whom you were sealed for the day of redemption.

There was good and bad news in this passage. Good news first—my eternal salvation is secured and sealed by the Holy Spirit. Bad news—I can grieve the Holy Spirit (aka, God) by corrupt talk. Seeming as I've struggled with my temper, I had undoubtedly, inexcusably spewed vile speech from my mouth. These two verses haunted me. There it was—I can bring grief to God. Exactly what

I suspicioned, exactly what I hated myself for. I tried to look up the Greek definition of the word, thinking that maybe its Greek origin connoted less force than its English competitor. Nope. Nada. It only reinforced what I feared. The Greek word for grief conveyed the idea of deep sorrow and was likened to the pain brought on in childbirth. Oh great! How I wanted to take this verse out of the Bible! I wanted to lessen its definition, water it down a bit.

I wrestled with this for quite a while, so I decided to look into the Greek meaning behind the words *please, to please, pleasure,* and *pleasing*, and its uses within the New Testament. With my *Strong's Concordance* in one hand and my Greek dictionary in the other, I went to work. Unlike the English language, the Greek language will often have multiple nuances and meanings to a single word. It will also have separate Greek versions of the word, even if there is only one English translation. In the Greek language, there are seven words with which to express the English derivations of the word *please*. Word by word, reference by reference, I sorted each meaning of the word *please* and how it related to the context of its respective passage.

After analyzing each use of the derivation of the word *please* in all its New Testament passages, I noticed that when the Bible was talking about actions that please God, the authors of *Mounce's Complete Expository Dictionary* frequently point out two very specific observations:

When the Bible addresses actions (or the lack thereof) that we Christians take that displease God, it's referring to the displeasing behaviors that are a part of our old character. We have a new identity

(new character) in which we do not live out of our old ways of living

but have put on a new way of living. The author states that we no

longer have that old identity.

When we Christians are told of things that please God, God is

the one bringing to fruition this new character via the working of the

Holy Spirit. The authors adamantly explain that man is not capable

of doing or pleasing God without the power of the residing Holy Spirit.

The Holy Spirit is the seal and deposit within us securing our new

identity. This is what ensures pleasing actions before God. To please

God on our own is impossible [8]

So then the question remained: What if I don't do the specific

actions outlined in Scripture that please God (e.g., obeying parents,

showing godliness within the home, sexual purity, confession of

Jesus to others,)? What if I fail at these? What if I only partially fulfill

these? What if I, as a Christian, hurt another Christian? Does this

displease God? Or is God still pleased with me because I have the

Holy Spirit and Jesus as a buffer? Just because I have the Holy Spirit

sanctifying and regenerating me does not mean that I act perfect or

sinless. If it's possible to please God with these actions, then how is

it not also possible to displease Him by the lack of such actions?

I needed to look into the Greek definition of the word

displease. [9] The words *displease, displeased,* or *displeasure* are used

only four times in the New Testament (each time being translated

as "displeasure"). That is remarkably less than the word *pleasure.*

There were some occasions in the New Testament in which the

variation of the word *please* was negated (e.g., God was not pleased). However, in each of those cases, the context was a time before Christ or specifically with unbelievers who are still under the wrath of God. Also, there was no mention of God being disappointed with His beloved children. As I was comparing the words *please* and *displease,* I realized that the idea of an action being something that "does not please the Lord" is different than actually bringing "displeasure" to the Lord. Something that "does not please the Lord" conveys an action (or a lack of action) that falls short from God's desired plan or will. It's incomplete in a sense and has not been satisfactory enough so as to bring pleasure to the Lord. The ability to bring displeasure to the Lord conveys another meaning. In this case we can only add to God's fullness—not adding to His character but adding to His joy. This means that our actions or lack of actions have the ability to take away from God's joy and fullness. However, it's important to emphasize that joy should not be made synonymous with *please.* Pleasing conveys an idea of satisfaction or of being acceptable— almost resonating with the concept of wholeness. However, the word *joy*[10] in the New Testament is used in regards to human emotion. Humans feel joy or aspire to have joy amid the circumstances of life. Joy is not something God aspires to have, achieve, or maintain. The Bible does not seem to advocate the idea of detracting from the fullness of God or His joy. The "joy of the Lord" is understood as something that already exists as a promise to us as believers, ready for our receipt, not something God is trying to receive from us. *Joy* is bestowed upon men by God, not bestowed on God by men.

The Greek word for joy is very similar to the Greek word

charis,[11] which is used for the English word *grace*. Each word conveys this idea of a benevolent God extending to mankind something that only He can impart because it is from the fullness of Himself. Neither joy nor grace are things that humans can impart to God, for He is already full of both—these gifts are already an overflowing and outpouring of His fullness. It also does not appear that our actions detract from the joy of God, as this is not mentioned in the New Testament.

These realizations made me circle back around to the doctrine of impassivity. The word *impassibility* is the Greek word *apatheia*,[12] which connotes the idea being immune to the distress of suffering. It carries the idea that one cannot add to or take away from the happiness of God. It states that God loves out of "sheer abundance and self-sufficiency, not in order to receive anything in return."[13] God can love this way because of His ability to give us a type of love known as *agape*, which is an unconditional love not based on human actions. The following is a quote from Michael Horton's book, *The Christian Faith*:

> God delights in the work of his hands, in our fellowship with him, in our worship, and in the love and service we render to our neighbor. Yet God needs none of this for his own fulfillment. In fact, it is because he needs nothing that the love he shows to creatures is creative. It is not because God lacks emotion that he loves with freedom, but because he does not lack anything. God does feel, but not as one who depends on the world for his joy. God responds to our sorrows with compassion, to our sin with anger,

and to our obedience with delight. Yet he does so as a generous rather than as a needy lover.[14]

So the question must be asked, "Can God suffer?" Horton makes the point that "God's free decision to enter into creaturely history never threatens his essential transcendence. God is always 'other' even when he is near. God shares in the joys and sorrows of his people, but he is never overwhelmed by distress."[15] especially in such a way that He is rash in his judgments. This is the same concept as that which maintains Jesus can be tempted yet live a life without sin. God, in the same way, can experience wrath but always in love. Horton suggests that God does not live out of eternal suffering. Describing the Trinity, he asserts that they (the Father, Son, and Holy Spirit) "open themselves up to a covenantal relationship with free creatures. Affected by the world, they [the Trinity] are not affected in the same way as we are because they are not the kinds of persons that we are."[16]

And so this is what I concluded—there seems to be biblical support for the notion that we can please (as in bringing satisfaction but not necessarily joy) to God via our actions. There seems to be less biblical support that we can bring a lack of joy to God via our actions. So does that mean that God is indifferent to our actions? According to Scripture, the answer is "no." There are many passages in Scripture that discuss events in which God will judge not only unbelievers but believers as well. Hebrews 9:27 says, "And just as it is appointed for man to die once, and after that comes judgment." Every man will have to account for his actions before the Lord. Revelation 20:15 and Romans 2:5–11 (as well as other passages) speak of God sentencing people to either Heaven or Hell. However, there are other passages within scripture that discuss God's judgment over the actions specifically of believers. Below are a few of those passages:

1 Peter 1:16–17: But just as he who called you is holy, so be holy in all you do; for it is written: "Be holy, because I am holy." Since you call on a Father who judges each person's work impartially, live out your time as foreigners here in reverent fear.

2 Corinthians 5:9–10: So we make it our goal to please him, whether we are at home in the body or away from it. For we must all appear before the judgment seat of Christ, so that each of us may receive what is due us for the things done while in the body, whether good or bad.

Romans 14:10–12: You, then, why do you judge your brother or sister? Or why do you treat them with contempt? For we will all stand before God's judgment seat. It is written: "As surely as I live," says the Lord, "every knee will bow before me; every tongue will acknowledge God." So then, each of us will give an account of ourselves to God.

1 Corinthians 4:5: Therefore judge nothing before the appointed time; wait until the Lord comes. He will bring to light what is hidden in darkness and will expose the motives of the heart. At that time each will receive their praise from God.

These passages of Scripture clearly identify that Christians are not immune from judgment. The passages listed above are distinctly different from passages such as Romans 2:5–11 and Revelation 20:15, which address salvific judgment (pertaining to the gift of eternal life with God). That is a judgment between eternal damnation and eternal salvation. The four passages of Scripture listed above (1 Peter 1:16–17, etc.) are a judgment of holy versus unholy living. In other words, these passages pertain to the stewardship of this gift of eternal life given to mere mortals. What can be concluded is that our actions do not save us but do determine our reward. This is evident in parables such as "The Shrewd Manager" in Luke 16: "Whoever can be trusted with very little can also be trusted with much" and in Matthew 25:14–30, "The Parable of the Bags of Gold," in which the master applauds good stewardship by saying, "Well done, good and faithful servant! You have been faithful with a few things; I will put you in charge of many things. Come and share your master's happiness!" This parable reminds us that our actions matter in regard to reward and satisfaction but they do not diminish the joy or love God bestows upon His children. On this note, it is also important to remind ourselves that pleasure is possible only if one is truly considered His child, an heir to the riches of Christ. As discussed earlier, a person is unable to please God and will have a life that results in displeasure if they do not receive the Holy Spirit as their deposit. This receipt of the Holy Spirit is found only in those who acknowledge Christ as both Lord and Savior.

After reviewing all these verses, I determined that God's joy can be unaffected by human action. However, God can be pleased or experience a lack of pleasure with our actions, which is a very different matter than God being displeased with our identity. Since we as believers are considered coheirs with Christ, adopted sons and daughters covered by the atonement of Christ's blood, God is fully satisfied with our personhood. Therefore, God can be simultaneously pleased with us as individuals while we are in the midst of human actions that don't necessarily please Him. This is the same concept of hating the sin but loving the sinner (Jude 22–23).

Last, and perhaps most importantly, although our actions, not our personhood, can cause grief to the Lord, we must understand that grief is a love word. By that I mean you can't be grieved by something that has no value to you. You are grieved because you love. So it is with God. And when actions that bring about grief are committed, it is necessary, healthy, and healing to repent. This restores fellowship. Although God doesn't move away from us even after the grief we cause Him, our sin moves us away from Him. But repentance and forgiveness restore a Spirit-filled relationship.

There are two things I have come to realize. Although I can cause grief to God because of my sin, 1) He still offers forgiveness over and over and over and over again, and 2) God also grieves when someone hurts me. We have a God that feels. Only a little while ago I was dismayed by this thought; now I am grateful for it. God loves each of us equally, to the extent of dying so that each of us could be with Him forever. When I hurt someone—a coworker, my family, a stranger—God hurts. But the grand reversal is that when someone hurts me, God hurts, as well. He is a God that feels. He is a God who extends compassion. He is a God who enters into the cavernous pit of pain with us so that we're not alone.

One of my favorite verses is Zephaniah 3:17. It was given to Israel as a prophetic promise of the New Covenant established through Christ. This verse is a profound reminder of the magnificent, complex, mysterious, empathetic, emotional, forgiving, and powerful God with whom we commune:

> The Lord your God is with you,
> the Mighty Warrior who saves.
> He will take great delight in you;
> in his love he will no longer rebuke you,
> but will rejoice over you with singing.

When you live in the reality of this type of love, you become a force to be reckoned with. A purpose and passion are ignited within you. You make God sing. You bring God delight. You are the apple of His eye and the song in His Spirit. Don't let the Enemy tell you anything different.

Chapter 11

"Someday" as a Noun

I keep waiting for "Someday." That allusive "Someday." Someday, when life isn't so hard. Someday, when I have more money. Someday, when I'm not that busy. Someday, when I get married. Someday, when I have kids. Someday, when I retire. Someday, when my house is paid off. Someday, when I get a chance to relax. Someday, when things are easier. Someday is like a dangling carrot. You chase and hope, falsely believing you might actually get a chance to appreciate it. But for some reason, it's never within your grasp. However, its possibility and potential seem so strong and so achievable that you continue to believe the lie that someday, life actually will get better. It's like you begin to believe that you'll enter some kind of reprieve, a rest of sorts, where bad things don't happen and pain and discomfort are minimal or not even present. I'm beginning to think that Someday really doesn't exist. Its arrival will always be pending but never complete. I think that Someday might be cousins with the tooth fairy or the Easter bunny. The belief in "Someday" provides momentary hope in which the dream deferred might actually step out of the shadows and come into fruition. If we categorize tough trials, momentary displeasure, and hopes for a better tomorrow into Someday, we have unknowingly denied the reality at hand in order to attempt to fix momentary discomfort.

I like the idea of "Someday." There are a lot of things I will do when I get to Someday. Someday always seems brighter and happier. It has a euphoric, satisfactory feel. Someday has been a Band Aid for many wounds, but Someday's adhesive is kind of poor. It falls off quickly, not giving me a chance to heal but deceiving me into thinking that I have. I succumb to Someday's lie fairly often; I'm quick to believe it. Not surprisingly, I find myself visiting again with its lofty ideas. But now, I'm catching on. Someday is bluffing me.

I've been thinking about eternity a little more lately. Two weeks ago my grandpa was diagnosed with lymphoma. One day he was fine, and literally two days later he was being rushed to the emergency room. And three days after that we got news that not only did he have cancer but that he only had weeks to months to live. Life changes so quickly. Within five days, Grandpa went from eating a Sunday lunch with us to being sentenced to death. The whole thing was very abrupt, a whirlwind of sorts. It came out of left field, with no warning and with no noticeable symptoms, really. And although Grandpa at this point (two and a half weeks later) is still with us, the Friday the oncologist told us the news was the day we already experienced a loss. A new reality began, and its heaviness has been daunting as we try to go forward.

We've shed so many tears in the last two weeks. I'm not ready to say goodbye to Grandpa. But who is ever ready for something like that? You're never really ready. You just have to deal with the misery. I told God that I didn't want to enter into this pain. I didn't want to deal with this situation—I wished it wasn't even a situation that existed. In my head, Grandpa is supposed to keep living and to be a part of family functions. I want to be in denial about his lymphoma. I want to claim that somehow the doctors are wrong. How I wish I could wake up from this horrible dream and know that everything is going to be alright. I know that we're fortunate he's lived a full life, but you're never really ready to say goodbye.

I hate death. I hate the finality of it all. I hate how memories are all that's left and that the future is cut off from your grasp. I hate the void it causes and the heartache that feels unquenchable. I hate seeing others who also cared deeply for this person melt as their hearts shatter. I hate watching someone physically and mentally fail—seeing their body shrivel up and waste away. I hate the curse of death. This earth is bound by it. I think that a part of the heartache comes when you realize there is so much love you have left to give, but the recipient can no longer receive it. It's a different form of unrequited love.

I have caught myself throughout this situation while thinking about Someday, when this is all over. It's hard to live through agony, so by default your heart and mind try to jump ahead to a place of stability, peace, and comfort. Someday shows up again, because in Someday, everybody is happy again, the sting of death has been soothed, and somehow you think the void will be filled. But as I began to entertain Someday's enticements, I discovered that Someday is not what I really want. Grandpa won't be around any longer Someday, so I really don't want to rush to get to that point in time. I want to soak up the time here and now that I have left with Grandpa. Yes, it will be painful, but I'm still blessed to have him around, the two of us living, breathing, laughing, and experiencing life together. When bad things happen, all *I think* I want is for things to go back to normal. I want to bypass the pain, and I want life's mundane routine with its trivial concerns to be my reality. I immediately tried to do that when I heard about Grandpa's diagnosis, but going back to a mundane routine with petty concerns was not really an option. The two options I discovered I had was to either embrace the moment I'm in now or to idly wait for Someday, when I have closure in the finality of death.

So here I am, two weeks out, still grieved by the impending loss but so grateful for every day I have left with Grandpa. Many people don't get time to say goodbye. They don't get time to make a few more precious memories or to get another hug and kiss. I've been given a gift, and I want to relish it. I can sit by in a stupor of grief, or I can allow the depth of my sorrow to remind me of the depth of my love for my dear grandpa. I want to love him like he's never been loved this side of eternity (which may be impossible, but it's worth attempting). I want to spend more time with him, make more visits, say more I love you's, and give more hugs. It may be grueling, it may take sacrifice, and it might get harder the more I see his body fail. But I have the privilege and honor to be with my grandpa. I don't want to miss this opportunity to keep on loving him.

Love is eternal. It is not bound by death, or time, or distance, or generations, or physical or spiritual life...it transcends all. It's a bond that no one or no thing has a right to break. Its connection runs deeper than blood. Life is eternal, as well. Jesus came to give people eternal life now, not just later. Eternal life doesn't begin after death. Eternal life begins with acceptance of the transcendent love of God—a love that pulls us out of the death-bound world into a place of intimately knowing and being known by the God "who gives life to the dead and calls things that are not as though they were" (Romans 4:17).

I was listening to a song by Gungor from their album called "Ghosts Upon the Earth." Michael Gungor was talking about the backstory of the album when he said, "Sometimes we think of these ideas like God and love and heaven and you know the ethereal ideas that we have as kind of the more ghostly, less concrete, real ideas and we think of ourselves as the concrete reality and this [album] kind of calls it into question and says what if we're more like the ghosts walking upon the earth longing to become real?"[17] When I read some of Paul's writings in Scripture, over and over again is this idea that life is not confined to this world. There is more to us. There is more to life. This is the foretaste—it wets our palate—but the true meal, the true heartiness of life, isn't found in what can be seen or touched—it is found in the eternal, intangible reality of the love of Jesus, which is present now and in the life to come. One of the songs in this album is called "This is Not the End." The lyrics say,

This is not the end
This is not the end of this
We will open our eyes wide, wider

This is not our last
This is not our last breath
We will open our mouths wide, wider

And you know you'll be alright
Oh and you know you'll be alright
This is not the end
This is not the end of us
We will shine like the stars bright, brighter[18]

The point is, this is not the end...passing from one life to another. Death is not the finality of living beings. Death is actually living in a transcendent form. For those who receive the love of Jesus, death is when we get ushered into a realm in which we are finally unhindered to be who we were really meant to be—full and complete, not held back by the sin or destruction of this world. Death is truly not death. Yes, it's death to this world, conclusiveness and a goodbye to the tangible reality we have only ever known. But it is also a welcoming of freedom from the curse that has entrapped the broken world. In a sense, death is almost a rebirth, a final rebirth, in which we now commune with the Creator and see face-to-face the one who loved us enough to die for us. It's where we become the purest form of our true selves.

Jesus spends so much time telling people about eternal life. He dedicates so much effort prying our fingers off the tangible, material, physical things that we've become so attached to in order that we're free to grasp onto what transcends all these temporal surroundings. Because Jesus knows this temporal life won't get better. It has ebbed and flowed between heartache and joy, and it will continue to do so. When we focus on life, the one we are involved in everyday—the one with bills, traffic jams, birthdays, and weddings—we get tossed about like a wave on the ocean. We experience highs and lows—utter pain and darkness and then euphoric, cloud-nine, million-dollar moments. But when we focus on eternal life, the one Jesus offers—the one with faith, surrender, hope, forgiveness, grace, and love, *rich unequalled godly love*—we become like the horizon on the ocean. Everything else is moving, storming, and roaring, yet eternal life is the clear line, the peaceful, guaranteed state of clarity, direction, and orientation. I love the phrase in the Gungor song that says, "And you know you'll be alright" because I finally am starting to get it. It will be all right, whether in life or in death, because my life, my identity, my joy, and my love do not cease when I exit the world. My life (eternal life) bridges the gap between this world and the next. And the next world is the place where the curse of this world can no longer restrain me. In death are we only fully alive.

So right now, during the car drives and the lunch breaks, in the quick texts and the late phone calls, in the grief of knowing I have to stay goodbye to Grandpa, and while completing the mundane task of grocery shopping, eternal life is already offered and can already be received. Here I am trying to find Someday, and Someday is right now, today. Here I am waiting for peace and rest, and peace and rest are offered right now. In and around the temporal is the greater reality of eternal life. Jesus is found in all these small places, in the places and things not confined to a church. So although Someday is usually thought of as a day in which this temporal life becomes better, the only form of Someday that can be counted on is what we know as eternal life, which is available *today*. True life isn't for "Someday." True life is the purest form of "Today"—it is the place where peace is found in chaos, where hope is found in despair, where forgiveness is found in the mess, and love is found past the feeling. Someday should be, and can be, experienced now, not just wished for like a belated Christmas present.

Life is not tomorrow or the next event. Life is right now. And knowing that is bringing me some comfort and hope. "Take hold of the life that is truly life" (1 Timothy 6:19).

Chapter 12

Untouched

One snowy Sunday evening in early December, I was trying a new recipe to make deep-fried, jelly-filled doughnuts—*ponchiks*. I thought to myself, *This is a simple one. If I like them, I could see myself making these all the time, maybe even for Christmas.* The recipe called for me to bring 24 ounces of oil to 350 degrees. I didn't have a thermometer, so I thought I could just bring it to a boil. I called my mom for some helpful hints. After all, her cooking is superb, and if ever I need some assistance with food, I ask her input. She told me to keep an eye on the oil because it can quickly get out of hand. Following her wise advice, I got everything ready and laid out. Fill dough with jelly. Check. Mix cinnamon and sugar together. Check. Spoon, plate, oven mitt...check, check, check. Now the oil. As I was on the phone with my mom, it started getting really smoky in the kitchen. Not thinking much of it because it's a small kitchen and has gotten smoky in the past when I'd fried something, I just opened the windows to reduce the smell. Soon, my fire alarm started to go off. *Great! This is embarrassing!* I didn't want the neighbors to think that something was wrong, because everything was under control. I informed my mom that my smoke detector was going off but that everything was fine. She suggested getting a cool towel and getting the smoke away from the detector. So I did. I glanced at my oil; everything was still fine. I meandered over to the fire alarm. After about 15 seconds, I came back, and, much to my horror, eight-inch flames were erupting from my pot. I screamed into the phone, "My pan's on fire!" In a split second, I had lost control of the situation. What had been fine was now volatile, and what had been just a gross smell had become a dangerous situation, all within the blink of an eye. In my panic, I grabbed a dirty cup from my sink, filled it with water, and threw it on the fire. I was expecting the fire to go out, but when water hit the blistering grease, the fire exploded at me (I did not realize you don't throw water on a grease fire). I can still hear the sizzle of the two elements meeting. I stood there in absolute panic as my life became tragically and despairingly changed in one catastrophic instant. The fire was so massive that it was as if it had become its own being, it had risen up in a wrathful fury, like some monster of incomparable size, and spat back at me. It took on its own life and breath, vehemently terrorizing me as I, only feet away, was held captive to its aggression. Before me arose from a two-quart saucepan a four-foot wide column of pure flame—consuming my cupboard, curling as the fire met my ceiling, and with flaming arms spread over my archway and down my hall. The wall behind my stove began to peel off, dissolving like ice in a warm drink. The screens in open windows behind me couldn't withstand the furious burst of heat and began to melt. Hot grease splattered across the room pitting my linoleum floor. My poor mother could only hear me screaming and crying as I was witnessing the calamity that was unfolding in my kitchen. She thought I had said that I was burning and had no other understanding aside from the background noises of fire and screaming. Apparently, I'd dropped my phone during the explosion.

My first thought, as I stood trapped there in the blazing inferno, was, *I've always thought this would be one of the worst ways to die—here we go!* The room was darkened, the breaker had blown, and when the fire hit the ceiling, only the light over the sink remained in the kitchen. As I stood in the shadow of the glowing flames and watched the blaze rage out of control, I started to think how painful this was going to be. The fire was threatening my life as it draped across the archway, my exit. I paused in shock, gathering my senses; out of fear, I ran under the flames to go get help. I pounded on my neighbor's door until she opened it. I asked if she had a fire extinguisher—to my dismay, she didn't have one, either. She called 9-1-1; my phone was lost somewhere in my kitchen.

I went back inside my home—my laptop was sitting on my dining room table, only feet from the fire. It seemed even more important because it held my book—this book. The book I'd been creating, pouring so much energy and love into, was sitting there just waiting to be consumed. You can't recreate what has already been formed, rewrite what has already been spoken. Why didn't I have this book backed up in a safe place? I feared that the completed chapters would soon vanish. I tried to go back into the kitchen to grab my laptop, but the flames were too intense. My laptop was only two to three feet from me but yet seemed far out of reach. I stood under the archway, screaming and sobbing. I remember screaming to my mother, who was at the other end of my lost phone, wherever it was, "I'm okay, I'm okay!" But those words she never heard. I think by that point she was already in the car on her way over. I remember watching the wall being stripped away with flame, hearing the fire's crackle that soon deafened my ears, and standing under the archway, seeing flames literally spitting out from the stove and wall. It was sickening, and I had the most horrific sinking sensation as I attempted to defy the reality before me, "This isn't my life! This can't be my life! This can't be happening!" I left my place again, realizing that I couldn't just idly sit by and watch my home burn to the ground. I needed to do something while I waited for the fire department to arrive.

I left behind my laptop, my book, my house, and all my possessions and sentimental treasures. I ran out the door, wearing only my slippers, socks, sweatpants, a long-sleeved shirt, and Grandma's blue and white striped apron. I didn't have time to put shoes or a coat on. I couldn't even chance getting my purse, or I might not be able to get back out of my house. In socks and slippers, I sprinted to another neighbor's house in four to six inches of snow. I pounded on their door, desperate to find a fire extinguisher. A lady, dressed in a housecoat and nightgown, peered through her window. Yelling, I asked if she had a fire extinguisher, and she shook her head "no." It felt like with every minute that passed, more of my place was being overtaken by fire. I quickly glanced around my neighborhood. Across the other side of my house, a small distance away, was a house with glowing Christmas lights. I knew these neighbors were home, so I began to run toward their house. The snow was heavy on my feet; I'd pulled off my slippers in my neighbor's driveway and was left with only my sopping-wet socks when I started my way to the other neighbor's house. As I ran, I fell in the snow. I'm not one prone to falling, but I couldn't catch my balance as I slid in the snow. I hurried and got back to my feet. Time was of the essence. I began to run again, and again I fell. This time I landed flat, dead-center in the middle of the street. I couldn't believe it. The house seemed to keep moving farther away. I remember thinking that I wasn't going to make it to the house: *I'm going to get hit by a car before I make it there.* I got up again and tried to run. I was ready to throw up, between the running and the adrenaline. I walked to the neighbor's front door, beating on it until the wife appeared in her housecoat. I asked for a fire extinguisher, and she had one! I felt some hope. Her husband brought it to her, and she struggled to get the door open as she tried to quickly unlock the handle. I pulled the extinguisher's trigger for a test-try on my way back to my house. As I ran back to my apartment, I heard the echoing sirens of the approaching fire trucks. It was such a surreal and eerie feeling to know that those sirens were coming for me—for nobody else but me! I was filled with a combination of thankfulness and deep sadness. What was happening to my world? What had I done?

By the time I made it back to my apartment, my living room was pitch black. I couldn't even see my front door through the screen door. I saw a small orange ball of fire piercing through the blackness. I was too late. I thought that the fire had already begun to devour my living room. At that point, I couldn't open my door. I was afraid I would only pull more flames out toward me rather than fight off further damage. Defeated, I stepped back from the flames. I remember standing on my snow-covered sidewalk in wet socks, still wearing my apron, staring up at the heavens and just crying, "Oh God! Oh God! Oh God!" Guttural moaning expressed the ache within—I so scared, so shocked, and so desperate for God to fix it. I thought that I had lost—or at least was in the process of losing—everything, every single thing except what I was wearing. I was so grateful to have my life but was agonizing over the very plausible prospect that all my belongings had been destroyed.

Three cop cruisers, two fire trucks, and an ambulance came. Although time seemed to hold still, they responded to the call very quickly. I've never been so happy to see a policeman or a fireman in my life. Some compassionate officer whisked me away, out of the cold and into a cruiser. The elderly lady who lived in the other half of the duplex and had called 9-1-1 sat with me in the back seat of the squad as the officers asked me what happened. I remember feeling so upset that just recalling my name seemed to be a challenge. I kept asking if my mom was there. It's strange, no matter how old you get, you still want your mom. All I wanted was my mom. I wanted to feel her loving arms hug me and make me feel like everything was going to be okay. I was so afraid that she was going to have a heart attack from the sheer panic and grief that she'd experienced while audibly witnessing me, her only child, in the midst of a catastrophe. At this point, she didn't know whether I had survived the fire.

I remember seeing the fireman getting the hose ready and thinking, *Hurry, please go faster.* The cop drove me to the ambulance, and I was told that my mother had just gotten there. I poured out of the cruiser and fumbled right into her arms. We both stood there for a few seconds, both of us sobbing uncontrollably before the officer directed me into the ambulance. My dad finally made it to the scene once we were in the ambulance; he hadn't been home when everything had gone down. It's such a comfort to see your loved ones when your world is falling apart. I sat in the ambulance, convulsing from the cold and adrenaline, coughing and crying—I was a dazed mess. Discussions of smoke inhalation, oxygen levels, and heart rates commenced. At that point, the realization of my protection finally hit. I'd been untouched. I'd suffered no smoke inhalation and remarkably...no burns, absolutely no burns. The paramedic remarked, "She's a lucky girl."

After a short stay in the ambulance, it was time to reenter the war zone. The smell of the smoke hit me like a brick wall. The smell was nauseating, nearly causing me to choke. As I stepped through my front door and walked into my kitchen, the haunting sounds of Christmas music on the radio were blaring. Only an hour before, that music was a representation of my holly jolly Christmas baking mood, and now it was an eerie reminder that my life had nearly been taken. I turned the corner, and my stomach sunk. My curtains had melted from the intense heat, black soot coated the ceiling, and my stove—I was caught between sobbing and throwing up—my stove was blackened and burned, knobs melted, and pan split. My refrigerator was scorched; my cupboards above the stove were torched. On top of the cupboards above my stove, I'd just put up Christmas garland and a snowman I had made earlier that afternoon with my mom. The garland was gone; the only thing that remained was my snowman, proudly standing as if to say, "I survived." His little scarf and hat were burned off, and his pure white surface was tainted with coal-colored scum.

Standing in the ruin, good news graced my ears. The fire was contained to the kitchen, having burned itself out; since it was a grease fire, the fireman didn't have to use water. Not only had I been shielded from being burned, nearly everything else I owned had also been shielded. And my laptop... survived...remarkably in the fire but yet untouched. That cold Sunday night changed my life. God's protection was absolutely astounding, and even now I don't understand how, aside from His good grace, I hadn't gotten burned.

The weeks that followed were far from easy, but yet much easier than they could have been. The first week I went into a mild shock. Sore from my falls for the next few days, my right leg ready to give out when I stepped down, unable to sleep, hearing what I thought was a fire alarm in the night, dreaming of flames—I was shaky and dazed. Although mentally I was struggling, physically I was unscathed—such a small price to pay—praise be to my Protector. Week two post-fire I was informed that I was liable for all damages, despite the fire being an accident. I was held responsible for full reimbursement of all the structural renovation, cleaning, and restoration. The cost was estimated to range from ten thousand to fifteen thousand dollars. My clothes and all the items in my place had to be professionally cleaned and were all smoke-damaged. Weeks three and four post-fire entailed battles between the insurance company, the landlord, and cleaning and restoration contractors, as the clean-up and repair commenced. It would be three months before I could return to my apartment.

In some regards, the entire experience evoked a disorienting sense of exile. It's the most surreal feeling to be wandering around your neighborhood in socks, running in the snow trying to save something that is essentially out of your control. It's the weirdest feeling to go from having all your needs met to thinking that all you own is what you're wearing in a matter of thirty minutes. It's bizarre to gather a few items here and there in plastic bags just to take them with you for who knows how long. It's an odd sensation to have your private haven laid open for strangers and cleaners to root through and discard, gather, or sort without your input. I had moved out of my parents' home to become independent and self-sufficient but quickly found myself at the mercy of and dependent on other's assistance, in particular my family. My possessions remained inaccessible for a number of weeks. There were incessant conversations about the daunting anticipation of removing, reorganizing, rebuying, and re-establishing. All these emotional and financial factors, without a doubt, proved to be challenging, but, truly, it was all a very, very small price to pay in the realization that I still had my life, my health, and my possessions. I was remarkably, unfathomably, inexplicably, most astoundingly...untouched. And my gratitude can't even be measured to the merciful God, who is very much alive.

There's so much I gleaned from the experience. I never, ever want to go through a life-endangering experience again—who does? In fact, the anxiety of suffering and pain continues to be one of my greatest fears. However, if I had to endure the experience, I might as well gain from it what God was teaching me. As I share what I learned, I hope that a tidbit or two resonate with you. The lessons I have learned and am continuing to learn thus far is as follows:

1. **NEVER put water on a grease fire.** I didn't know this important fact. Water plus a grease fire equals a near-bomb. Use only baking soda, salt, a fire extinguisher, or put a lid over the flames, if possible. Don't use flour; depending on the density of the flour, it, too, can create an explosion. Don't attempt to remove the hot oil and dump it out the window or into the sink. I've heard of others who have done so, which resulted in severe burns.

2. **Always have a working fire extinguisher.** Make sure that the extinguisher is charged. Over time, the tank can become empty. It's never good to find that out in the literal "heat" of the moment. It's kind of ironic. My parents were actually going to buy me a fire extinguisher at Christmas, only three weeks away. Now I have three fire extinguishers in my house. You can be sure I have one especially located in my kitchen. I never planned on having a fire. You never "plan" on having an accident. I've actually always taken extra precautions to avoid any electrical shortages or fire hazards. And yet I found myself roaming around my neighborhood desperate for someone to have an extinguisher.

3. **If you are a renter, always have renter's insurance.** Even if your landlord doesn't require it, even if you can't "afford" it, get it. If some catastrophe happens, you'll realize that you can't afford the expense that results from it. You'll quickly realize that renter's insurance doesn't actually cost that much when you compare it to restoration costs. (Also, insurance companies will often give you a discount on your car insurance premiums when you bundle renter's with car insurance.) I didn't purposely choose not to have

renter's insurance; I just didn't get around to it. I forgot, and thought I would get to it in the future. I didn't plan on being a "dumb" renter, but no one is immune to accidents. Yes, renter's insurance covers your stuff, but what I didn't know is that it also covers your liability. If I'd actually had renter's insurance at the time of the fire, I wouldn't have had a ten-thousand to fifteen-thousand-dollar bill for damages hanging over my head.

4. **Be open to others, even to those you wouldn't normally be open toward.** I didn't know my neighbors, aside from the elderly lady who called 9-1-1, prior to the fire incident. But the night of the fire, I was in dire need of their help. That night, all the walls came down. I didn't care what type of person they were, if we usually didn't talk when we saw each other, if they were complete strangers. I needed them, and all the cordial points of etiquette, such as "How do you do?" and "What's your name?" didn't matter. They were willing to help, and I was in desperate need of their assistance. I remember one sweet neighbor, whom I'd never met, came over in her boots, pajamas. and robe to the police cruiser I was waiting in and asked if I wanted to wait in her warm house. It's amazing how much of a friend a stranger can become. My neighbors were like an oasis in the desert. Usually, I dread—and even get mad—when I see a policeman on the side of the road waiting to pounce on a speeder; that night, the policeman felt like my best friend. I've never been so happy to see strangers in uniforms in my life.

5. **It's worth investing time and kindness in people.** Each person has their own strengths and weaknesses. What may

be one person's strength may be another's weakness and vice versa. I've grumbled and complained about people on more than one occasion. Some of these people were the same people who rushed in with support, either financially or emotionally, after my fire. It was humbling, to say the least. These people, whom I had judged for frustrating weaknesses, loved me when I didn't even deserve it. I've found that judging needs to stop. Yes, we are humans. Yes, we get on one another's nerves. Yes, we disagree and can be catty. But we have the choice to be the bigger person—to put aside judgments and accept others for who they are, to concentrate on their strengths even though we recognize their weaknesses, and, most importantly, to love them fully despite their flaws. Release the bitterness and grant forgiveness. People try our patience, but it's time to tame the tongue, not degrade their name or person by our words or even our thoughts. Sometimes I think we chalk up people to be either good or bad, annoying or cool, in or out; what I realized after the fire is that the categories don't matter. They need to be put aside.

6. **"It's not worth it."** This phrase kept running through my head over and over again after the night of the fire. Most things that I obsess, complain, get angry about, stress over, and try to control are simply...not worth it. Life is too short to be angry, especially angry over petty things. Time doesn't always deserve the importance I place on it. Traffic can wait. The list of "things to do" will get done when they need to get done. Who cares how people judge you? Who cares that you didn't get your hair perfect? It's not the end of the world that you missed your favorite sports team play on television, or that you missed the big sale at the grocery store this week. That

stuff doesn't matter. Everything isn't urgent or even necessary. The important things in life are people, family, friends, your health, and your relationship with God. These are the things that last and hold priceless value. So much of what we complain about really just needs to be let go. Sometimes we need a reality check, a pause, and a deep breath to realize that life could be so much worse.

7. **Bite your tongue a little more.** I have wasted so many words complaining, judging, being cynical, being sarcastic, and, sadly, at times even being foul. Why? How is that bettering my life or those around me? What's the point? I have so much more to be grateful for than I do to complain about. It's not worth making that funny, yet snide, remark just to "fit in." It's not worth tearing down someone else just to be in with the group. It's not worth harboring bitterness and blame when Christ has freed us to live beyond those entrapments. Sometimes it serves us better to withhold a thought or comment, even though the temptation to express it is great. Be slow to speak (James 1:19).

8. **For weeks following the fire, I remember being keenly aware of how truly rich I was.** I was, and am, abundantly blessed. It's so easy to get frustrated, to get upset by what we "don't have" that we miss all that we do have. I have so many blessings within reach every single day. Each day I'm grateful that I'm not burned— that I'm not laid up in a hospital and paying burn-wound bills. I'm grateful that I can still work and still have the full use of all my appendages. Many people aren't that fortunate. Many people have endured life-endangering events, and even though they survived

those events, they lost so very much. I haven't. God has graced me with a second chance at life, and now I want to live it right. Not that I ever tried to live it wrong before, but there is a "reality check" this experience has brought. And although a part of me wants to forget it, at the same time, I don't believe I should. I want to keep the realization at the forefront of my mind that life is precious and a gift that could easily be taken from me. I'm not entitled to this gift, and I'm not entitled to each morning that I'm blessed to wake up. Everything I have is a plus. My life, right now, could be so different. And I praise God that the damage I have incurred is only financial, slightly emotional, and most assuredly redeemable. I'm beyond blessed.

9. **I can't speak for guys, but as a woman, there is this constant interpersonal dialogue about how you look.** You compare yourself to others and nitpick about all physical flaws. We're quick to complain about our imperfections and even quicker to base our value on such attractable or unattractive qualities. After the fire, I realized that I could have had both arms burned. I easily could have had my face scalded. I could have lost my sight, inhaled smoked, scorched my throat, or lost the use of my fingers. All of these painful life changes could have been real happenings. But, praise God, they were not for me. I may not be the most beautiful woman, and I may not like how short I am, how I look, or what my hair looks like, but my goodness, I'm not wounded. So I think the least I can do is be thankful for what I do have and what I do look like. The year I had my fire, I complained that I was going to be turning 25 years old, a whole quarter of a century. I was turning another year older and still

not married. But after my fire, I was so grateful for my twenty-fifth. That year, I themed my birthday party, "Alive and Twenty-five." It's a blessing to have a birthday.

10. **Share with others.** It's easy to keep track of what's yours, what's theirs, to hoard and protect our possessions and be stingy about giving. After the fire, so many people, especially my family, gave, gave, gave. I have borrowed and used many of my parents' things. My mom keeps saying that's what family does, and I understand that, but the point is, they don't at all keep track of all the stuff I've used. It makes me want to apply that same approach to all who borrow from me—to have a "what's mine is yours" attitude. People have been so generous; now, more than ever, I want to spread that same generosity. When people are in need, I want to give, even if I don't have much at the moment. I've been blessed again and again so deeply by all those who have given to me. I want to pay it forward and bless others like they've blessed me. It's time to quit keeping tabs, to let others go first, and to throw away the invisible scoreboard of rights and wrongs.

11. **Enjoy the gift of normalcy.** To wake up in the morning and have a "boring" day is sometimes a greater gift than we give it credit. When things go terribly wrong, all you long for is a day when life feels normal and mundane. Suddenly, the ordinary looks extraordinary. Two weeks after the fire, my mom got sicker than I had seen her in over a decade. It hit right at the holidays. Mom was sick, plans were rearranged, and I found myself in my apartment on Christmas Eve cleaning out my once-organized draws and stowing

the contents in a giant, disorganized box in preparation for the cleaners who were coming that following Monday. It was odd. I was there only an hour, but it felt long and strange, hearing the tired smoke detector chirp as the battery died. I was ever so careful not to brush against a wall so as to avoid covering my clean coat in greasy soot. It was empty and dark. Life felt unnervingly "not right." The simple things seemed like a desperate longing. I just wanted normalcy—I wanted my mom's health to get better, I wanted my apartment to be restored, I wanted my daily, run-of-the mill routine back. So, I encourage you to be grateful for what you have now, because one day, maybe even sooner than you thought, it could all be taken from you.

12. **Show kindness to all, especially to those who are hurting.** I can't tell you how much texts, phone calls, or a simple "How are you doing with everything?" really meant to me. Many people donated money, donated time, and donated listening ears, all of which touched me deeply to the core. I knew that people cared, and just a kind word or encouraging note gave me enough grace to remind me that life was still very good despite the chaos around me. So when someone you know, even if you don't know them that well, is going through a difficult time, take time to show them you care. Send a card, lend the money, give them a call, tell them you are praying for them, or simply ask how they're holding up. It really does help.

13. **God hasn't promised to prevent the "fire," but He has promised to stay with us during the "fire."** I believed this in the

metaphorical sense—never really thought I would know it in the literal sense. This experience has just further confirmed that belief. There are difficult situations that, unfortunately, God doesn't shield us from; however, He promises to never leave or forsake us (Hebrews 13:5). He'll walk with us during the trials. I felt a little like Shadrach, Meshach, and Abednego in Daniel 3:13–30. I was not spared from the experience, but I was shielded from the inferno.

> So Shadrach, Meshach and Abednego came out of the fire, and the satraps, prefects, governors and royal advisers crowded around them. They saw that the fire had not harmed their bodies, nor was a hair of their heads singed; their robes were not scorched, and there was no smell of fire on them. (Daniel 3:26–27)

Could I be any more fortunate?

I think back over that night, replaying the line of events. I should have gotten burned. I shouldn't have made it out unscathed. I could easily have had my face over the hot oil. If the disruption of the smoke and the detector had not occurred, I might have been turning down heat or stirring the pan. It distracted me for 10–15 seconds, which in turn kept me from being the recipient of the flash fire that broke out during that time. On the floor, only inches from where I was standing that night, were burn marks embedded into the linoleum. I can't help but wonder, if the fire caused that much damage to the floor, how much more mutilation could it have caused to my skin? Subsequent to that chilling thought is the question of pure amazement, "How did I not get burned?"

There's so much to internalize about the situation, but I'm grateful for the new chance at life. Sadly, the common frustrations of daily living will vie for my attention. Taxes and rising gas prices become bigger deals than they need to be. But I want to try to remember the way I felt during the weeks following the fire and not lose my head to the complaints that so quickly flow from my heart. Every day is a gift. I know that's a cliché, and, usually, I'm opposed to all clichés, but this phrase has become a reality to me. Life is too short to waste it on the things that don't matter. There's much to do and much to experience. So if you've been blessed with a new day, live it up. Sing! Dance! Rest! Smile! Give! Learn! ENJOY! God is so good!

Chapter 13

The Third Entity

I was reading C. S. Lewis the other day. If that man wasn't dead, I would love to meet him. How invigorating would it be to sit at a little round table near Oxford discussing life, God, and all the deep matters of the vastness of the spirit while sipping hot coffee or perhaps a spot o' tea? The conversation would probably start off promising, common ground (yes, God exists, the earth is round, and coffee is very good, indeed), and soon my finite mind would get twirled and spun, twisted and lost in the brilliance of the intellectual apologetic. I think that I would leave both energized and drained, inspired and yet defeated from marveling at his genius—certain only of my name and that I like decaf. For Lewis, I assume it had to be nearly as much a curse as it was a blessing to think as deeply and philosophically as he did. But his processing penned for all to read has satisfied many a soul searcher's thirst for mental stimulation and, ultimately, truth.

I was reading *A Grief Observed*, in which Lewis processes the death of his beloved wife. I believe the book had to be written only weeks after her death—the freshness and raw emotion pierced the pages and cut to the deepest part of the soul, where heartache is held. He does not hold back. A man known for his advances in uncovering more clarity on the true nature of God pours out guttural cries of despair and doubt. The book is truly intense, but yet so real. You can't help but be captivated by his honest evaluation of such anguish. At one point in the book, Lewis writes concerning his wife's death,

If God's goodness is inconsistent with hurting us, then either God is not good or there is no God: for in the only life we know He hurts us beyond our worst fears and beyond all we can imagine. If it is consistent with hurting us, then He may hurt us after death as unendurably as before it.[19]

I read that, paused, and then began to underline it. If you were to be truly honest, honest with yourself to the point where it almost scares you, you're left staring at that statement and realizing either one, you've totally felt that way before, or two, you currently still do. And then comes the chill down your spine.

This world is so painful. Oh yes, life is good, so very good—at times almost euphoric. But at other times, it feels like an everlasting funeral service, full of tears and sorrow. Sometimes I feel as if my heart can't hold all the pain that pervades the millions walking a misfortunate path. I just want to fix it all, heal everyone from their heartache. and restore what it is they've lost and long for back into their trembling hands. Tonight I was talking with a friend on the phone, recounting all the tragic sad stories that have laid heavy on my heart the past couple weeks. Yesterday, I had a man come in for a medical test to see if his cancer had progressed. As I was prepping him for his exam, the man, without prompting, began sharing about his wife, who had died in that very same hospital ten years prior. The pain of his loss had left a wound so wide that speaking about it a decade later brought the gruff man to unrestrained tears. He went on to tell me that his son had also died in an auto accident within the last few years. I felt so helpless and grieved by this man's load. He had lost his wife, lost his son, lost his health, even lost part of his lung—and now was losing his money to his health, which he'd just learned was worse than he'd thought. What more could he handle? I just stood there, unable to say anything else except "I'm so sorry," just longing to make his life right again. Another man in my church has been by his wife's bedside, caring for her as she slowly slips into eternity. They've been married for 67 years; even in her weakness, when asked if she remembers her wedding day, her tired face glowed as she smiled and said, "I will never forget that day." Just a few weeks ago, a young girl recalled a story about an accident that she and her friend had been in when they were around sixteen years old. I figured she was referring to a fender bender, which in itself is an unnerving experience, but as I asked a few more questions, I came to discover that the accident was severe. The girl made it out of the accident with a broken wrist, but her friend wasn't so lucky. She endured something much more horrific—she was left a quadriplegic. I sat there affronted by the cruelty of life. Sixteen and a quadriplegic all from an innocent drive one very black evening. I can't help but wonder if that adolescent, once beaming with dreams, goals, and ambitions, felt trapped in her new reality. The life that she'd once had was stolen from her—it would never be the same. This unfortunate young girl watched her friend walk away and move on with life, able to have boyfriends, graduate from high school, attend prom, drive wherever she pleased, experience the common joys of being a teenager, go to the college of her choice...achieve all the dreams she'd set forth to achieve. Meanwhile, she lay with her life nearly taken from her, unable to feed herself, let alone write a note, unable to feel her feet touch the ground or experience the simple pleasure of walking across the room, discovering that her college selection was limited and her choice of degrees even more restricted. She probably lay wondering if her future held the possibility of a husband or kids. That girl lost so much, so very much. Sixteen, and her promising hope of a future came crashing down like a house of cards. I'm almost moved to tears as I think about it now. It's too much to bear as a bystander. Oh God bless that suffering girl for all she's overcome as a victim.

Sometimes grief just overtakes you and your hollow, bleeding heart despairingly agonizes, "Oh world, I cannot bear your torment!" How can a loving God allow such atrocities? How can an all-seeing Father allow His children to walk into the pits of hell? How can a God who is considered good withhold His intervention at the time you needed Him the most? How? Why? Does anybody care?

After my fire, I remember shaking hands with a man at church. He asked me about the fire, and I was quite quick to claim specifically that God had protected me from the flames. I did not waver and, without hesitation, attested all intervention to God. Only three years prior, almost to the date, this faithful man of God had lost his 13-year-old son to a long, slow, and very painful death to leukemia. And the God to which he and the church had so fervently poured out prayer after prayer begging for healing was the same God that chose to intervene on my behalf. I couldn't help wonder, as I finished shaking his hand, if he thought to himself, "God, you spared her, but why didn't You spare my son?" Same God—to one He's the hero, to the other He's the betrayer.

I have spent years trying to add and subtract, reconfigure

and maneuver the misfortunes that besets seemingly undeserving individuals, including myself, in efforts to resolve life to be fair. But that is an evasive lie. This life is not fair, and neither is God. The lyrics of a Sara Groves song say, "I keep wanting You to be fair. But that's not what You said. I want certain answers to these prayers. But that's not what You said."[20] A fair God would always return evil for evil and good for good. Ya know, the ol' eye for an eye, tooth for a tooth deal. A fair God would make the rapist break his ankle as he fled from the site so that he would get caught. A fair God would allow the drunk driver to have brain damage instead of the innocent father of three. A fair God would let the murderer get stricken with stage 4 cancer instead of the young thirty-year-old. A fair God would have continued to protect the grandfather who made it through the triple bypass surgery remarkably and prevented the blood clot that killed him a month later. A fair God would have stopped the cancer, prevented the accident, healed the good guy, trapped the bad guy, and been there when you needed Him. Sometimes life feels like a sick joke or like you're living in the twisted ending of a horror film.

Many years ago, one particular summer proved to be especially challenging. I had spent the first month of the summer trying to paint a layer of Christian clichés and obligatory beliefs over my true emotions. It worked...for a month. And then I couldn't even muster up the strength to put on the fake smile and parade the false happiness. I was at the end of me and, quite frankly, at the end of God. The ceiling was removed, the walls had crumbled, and there I was on my knees crying, battered by the unrelenting rain of anger, betrayal, depression, and grief. Much of this anger was aimed at

God—the God who left me (or so I thought). I was in an odd sort of place. Although I didn't reject him, I was utterly and most deeply mad at Him for His lack of intervention in my life on a particular matter I had prayed so earnestly about. I spent much effort expressing to Him the constant betrayal I experienced as the God I had believed in for so many years seemed to abandon me over and over again. The more I called out, the more I felt that He'd left me. It made me sick—He came to those who didn't even want Him, while I felt as though He'd left me alone, cold, in a dark alley. Who was this God of love people talked about? I was becoming less assured that this God was the God of Christianity. While I was mad and doubting God, I couldn't stop talking to Him. But my words were not full of endearment. A lot of the "talking" should be redefined as "yelling," "questioning," and a pretty raw, intense, and angry formation of vocabulary. Although, I kept in constant communication with God as I sorted through the events unfolding, I shelved the religion of Christianity in order to take an objective view of all the major religions of the world. From my years of studying science, I knew there had to be a God, a Creator, but at this point, I was unconvinced that this God was the Christian God I had followed since I was five. I found myself in a despairing, depressing sort of state, like nothing I had experienced before. I believed in a God but wasn't sure if the faith that had raised me would be the faith I would continue to pursue, and I was confused by life's unfair cruelty. I spent hours, days, and months surveying other religions and wrestling in my prayer life with a God I wasn't sure was there or was true, while at the same time missing the God I used to know. If there was a loving God, and this loving God was the Christian God I had been worshipping, then why would this loving God refuse to intervene at the time I was so desperate for His intervention? If this Christian God was truly loving (despite feeling quite the opposite), how could I reconcile following a God who says He loves me but who allows such agony? In my eyes, if I chose to follow this God, it would be like a girl who stays with a bad boyfriend and continues to make excuses for him, claiming he is still good even when, in fact, he is not.

Nearly a year and a half later, I wrote the following in my prayer journal:

Dear God. So I came to this revelation (if you would call it that because I'm not even sure if it proves true) today. It goes as follows: Life deals us crap. You don't deal us crap. But crap happens in life. It's a terrible world in so many ways, but it's not because You made it that way; it's because of the consequence of sin and of the Fall. So, in light of that, what You do is let the crap happen because, in truth, that's what we asked for with our own free will. Because You love us and You want a true relationship with us—not a robot relationship but a relationship with ebb and flow, wooing and calling, chasing and desire, you allow us to exercise our free will. And since this world is not as it is supposed to be, the wicked prosper, the righteous die a fool's death (just as Ecclesiastes talks about), illness is rampant, dreams are unfulfilled, and people suffer. It's the product of free will, it's the product of the Fall. And what You promise is not to give us what we want or to even fulfill what our dreams are, but what You do promise is to work everything for good for those who love You. Because of all this crap, because of billions of people's free will and all the chaos constantly happening because of the Fall, we can't realize why we can't always get what we want, but You, for those who love you, are making everything work out for the best, the best it possibly can be despite the circumstances, despite the crap, despite the free will...because I love You, you are going to make things work out for the good, despite the crappy answer and the unfulfilled dreams! So I'll take this "revelation" for now and see if it holds true to life and to Your character. Thank you, God, for being in the business of restoration. In Jesus name, amen.

This "revelation" was pivotal. I still was undone in so many ways, but I finally started to turn a corner—to reconcile the grief of this world with a loving God. I've never forgotten that journal entry because in many ways it has helped me cope with other challenging experiences. That day I realized that there was a third entity in the mix, and it was called "life." Although life is not a living, breathing force like God or Satan, it is what we all experience, are surrounded by, and partake in. Realizing that this third entity took some of the blame off God, I could see how God might actually be loving. In life, we experience much pain and tragedy. I think we all can agree on that, no matter how perky you may be. However, this is not God doling out tragedy like an evil witch casting spells; rather, the tragedy is the consequence of living in a bent and sinful world.

God is not fair; however, He is just. Because He is a just judge He allows consequences for the fallen nature of this world. Adam and Eve, in the original sin, chose on behalf of all human kind to break the right, perfect, unified relationship and environment with God. This sent not only man, but all of creation, spiraling into a broken, impure, tainted new reality. I had a professor that once stated something to the effect that "the rest of Bible, after the Creation story, is God reclaiming His world and trying to make things right again." Because of God's character, He is stuck between a rock and a hard place as He reclaims the world. God is fully love, but He is also fully holy. In Scripture, the use of the word *holy* often connotes the meaning "separate" or "other than." God does not simply contain these qualities, as we as Christians contain the quality of compass for the sick, etc., but rather He *is* love and He *is* holy. These qualities are what He embodies—they are His identity. So how does a holy God connect with an unholy people when the love that He carries for these people continually beckons Him to be united with them? That is the grand, overarching story of the Bible—a perfect God wooing imperfect people back to Him in perfect unity, as it once was.

Since God is stuck in this conflicting position, He must enact justice while enacting love. Key to this conflict is humankind's free will. God does not want love given to Him out of obligation or duty, but rather He desires freely given love. It's the same as a couple who gets married. The wife longs to be desired by her husband just as the husband longs to be wanted by his wife. The feelings of the two should naturally overflow for one another. God is like a lover wooing us, His beloved. So wouldn't a wise lover give only good gifts? Any young woman would be thrilled if the guy she was dating bought her flowers all the time, wrote her sweet love letters, spoiled her with diamond jewelry and fancy dinners, always sent text messages saying he was thinking about her, opened doors for her, gave back massages, took her on expensive shopping sprees, and listened intently to everything she said. That man would be the man of her dreams, and of course she would marry him. So if God wants to woo us, why does He allow such disappointment? Shouldn't our perpetual happiness always be His highest goal?

If the entirety of my love for my husband was based on all he did and not on who he was, our marriage would be short-lived. What if I became bored with the roses, the texts started to seem redundant, and the back massages were just as commonplace as the routine of going to work, then what he did would no longer be enough. I need to enjoy who he is, who we are as a couple, and appreciate our relationship and not just his abilities. Likewise, God does give good gifts. If you take an honest look at the blessings around you, you can't help at times feeling a little spoiled. If you live in America, you have clean running water (every day), you have food on the table, a warm house and a warm bed, the ability to drive, the freedom to vote, and even the freedom to worship when you want and how you want, despite your religious identification. So God does give good gifts, but what He gives may not always appear good.

Since God is just, He does have wrath in response to sin. When you're the one who has endured a wrongful offense, more than ever you want the wrath of God to be dispensed on the offender. And the more heinous the crime, the greater the vengeance you long for. If, however, you are the offender, the less you want to experience this wrath of God. Ah, yes, "beauty" is all in the eye of the beholder. Now, thankfully, Jesus was a propitiation of the wrath of God. By that I mean Christ became the atoning sacrifice, the appeasement and satisfaction for the wrath of God. Since God is holy He requires holiness, which a sinful human race was unable to accomplish. So God made a way, through the death of Christ, to satisfy His wrath so that those who are covered by the blood of Christ will receive only God's grace, love, and forgiveness. This allows God to do what He's been desiring to do since the Garden of Eden—be close to us, and in return for us, those who accept His offer of forgiveness, to be close to Him. I digress. This subject is so deep and so involved that simply outlining in it in a couple sentences may risk causing more confusion than good. However, for the sake of some clarity, I felt it necessary to at least highlight the matter.

Moving on. I say all this to emphasize that God must stay true to His character, which is both fully loving and fully holy. When Adam and Eve caused the upheaval in all of cosmology, God was placed in a position in which He must enact justice while also bestowing love. He is just, but He is not fair in the sense that He does not treat us as our sins deserve. So although He doesn't strike the murderer down with lightening, He also withholds His "fairness" towards us—for our vulgarity He should burn our mouths; for our eyes observing unwholesomeness, He should blind us, etc. His "unfairness" can be a rather convenient thing, when we realize that He provides us with grace rather than balancing of the scales. Sometimes double standards aren't so bad after all.

I used to believe in a micromanaging God. The one who had some sort of direct influence on the color of shirt I wore, the placement of furniture and particular guidance as to what food I ate and the precise bite I took. I used to believe that God's hand played a part in every single detail, even down to the spacing of holes found on a button. As you can imagine, for a person who thinks a lot, this has compounding and crazy effects. If God finely orchestrated when and how tall every shade of grass may grow or how many times a person blinks, then He must be to blame for everything, whether good or bad. I don't know if I've ever believed that God didn't care, but I have believed that He cares too much. I've often said that I believe God gets both too much credit and not enough credit. Countless times in my life I've heard people say that God did this, or God did that, or God's going to strike you with lightening, etc. I've been guilty of the same verbal acclamations. But in that kind of talk, it is very obvious that those speaking picture a capricious God, with a quick temper ready to *cause* specific circumstances. It's a picture of a God who moves us around like pawns on a chess board. Checkmate!

I now believe in a "macro" managing God. I believe that He's a God who is, in many ways, "hands-off" yet intimately involved in the lives of people, which leads me back to the third entity, called life. In life, there is a set of natural physical laws and scientific constants (e.g., the law of gravity, the law of thermodynamics, the speed of light, $E=mc^2$, etc.). These laws govern the universe. They were set at the dawn of creation, and because of their surety, we have a stable habitat in which we creatures, called humans, can survive and dwell. Because of science, I can't deny that there is a Creator, and after years of searching, skepticism, doubting, and intellectual digging, I can only conclude now with absolute certainty that this Creator truly is the triune God Christians worship.

This environment in which we dwell is stable, but it is not perfect. Thus, DNA does not copy correctly, causing genetic defects; entropy persists, so aging and death must occur; pollution fills the air, viruses hijack cells, bacteria mutates, and therefore death, disease, and disorder victimize the human race. This is not divine intervention, but natural effects on a natural world that has been spoiled by sin. Many happenings, whether good or bad, can't always be blamed on God. I don't believe that God strikes a person with cancer or causes the accident. Those are the outcomes of the laws of nature while adhering to the rules by which they play. If God is not the direct cause of specific misfortunate events, then, in the same light, He is also not the direct cause of specific good events. In the book, *The Language of God,* by Francis Collins, he defines miracles as, "an event that appears inexplicable by the laws of nature and so is held to be supernatural in origin."[21] He goes on to explain how many medical phenomena may appear to a lay person as "miracles" but can be explained as the proper workings of natural law. For a simplistic example, if a person catches a cold, it's no miracle or direct intervention by God that after a week or two, he or she is cured of their cold. The body is designed to have white blood cells that fight the infection and filtration processes to rid the body of its toxins. This is the proper set-up and the expected outcome. Collins goes on to have an in-depth discussion explaining Bayes' theorem and the probability theorem. Simply put, these two theorems suggest that certain events (whether good or bad) may occur because of the probability of their occurrences. Whether that is a high or low probability, the fact is that it's probable the event could and will occur. So although the event may be rare, it may not be miraculous.

To be honest, it seems kind of wrong to not attest to God accolades for all the blessings. But if we were to attest to Him praise for every good thing and blame for every bad thing, then wouldn't we again be making Him a cosmic puppeteer? In the same respect, if we remove blame from God based on probability and the laws of nature, should we also remove praise? Here, though, is the clarification: God is the giver of life, the giver of every good thing. James 1:17, "Every good and perfect gift is from above, coming down from the Father of the heavenly lights." He is not the giver of death, nor the giver of every bad thing. That becomes the role of the third entity, life, and more importantly the role of Satan, the thief. The one which John 10:10 says has come "only to steal and kill and destroy."

God is the Master Designer. He has set the laws in place and created an atmosphere where humans and other life forms live symbiotically with the environment surrounding them. There is a harmony in the intricacy of the grand design. It is as if God is the owner and creator of a factory. In that factory, He has set up machines and specific jobs for each part of the assembly to build the product. The machines and jobs established are self-sufficient. Although God monitors and is aware of all that is occurring in the factory, He does not directly maneuver each machine each time it runs. He sets up its function when He first began the factory, and so production carries on seamlessly without His direct input but under His supervision. The laws of nature function similarly. God is sovereign, and God is still God. He is Lord and ruler over all. Nothing goes on without His knowledge. Ultimately, God is in control. So there again lies a problem: If God is not the cause of the misfortune, He is still the one who permits it. Why would a good God allow such adversity?

I think a common misperception is that the highest level of human existence is happiness. We strive to be happy. We work hard at doing things and at setting up our lives in ways that would result in happiness. It's what we chase after, why we buy more goods, why we rearrange furniture, why we paint the walls, why we take vacations, why we eat dessert, why we climb the corporate ladder, and why we can close our eyes at night. We work hard to secure, maintain, and achieve positions, functionality, feelings, and materials so that, ultimately, we'll be happy. We live for pleasure. So when things don't go our way, and when our world comes crashing in, it contradicts and interrupts our striving for happiness. I believe God does want His children to be happy, although I don't believe that it's His ultimate goal for our lives. A good life in God's eyes is not a life in which His beloved are perpetually happy and not experiencing sorrow. A good life in this broken world, in God's eyes, is a life conformed to that of Jesus. You don't have to be a Christian to know that Jesus' life was not one of perpetual happiness. In fact, it was fraught with great adversity and persecution. If God allowed His very own Son to endure a smudged reputation, verbal attacks, temptation by Satan, a threatened life, and eventually a life that ended in brutality and physical and emotional torture, then why would we be immune to the same distress? Apparently, God's main concern is not our happiness or even our physical safety (which we will discuss further in the next chapter), but His main concern is with that of invisible qualities—a soul open, available, malleable, and effective in receiving, transforming, and proclaiming the everlasting love and grace He bestows. 1 Corinthians 11:32 confirms this idea: "Nevertheless, when we are judged in this way by the Lord, we are being disciplined so that we will not be finally condemned with the world." God would rather allow the difficulties now if that will prevent the damnation later.

I think God is grieved when we experience the heartache that scares us. When we're hurting, I think God also hurts. Although God seems to use difficult times to really work in our hearts, I don't believe that it's His preference. He created the world to be a beautiful paradise in which He would commune unhindered with His creation. Like a parent never "wants" to discipline their child but rather needs to out of love for them, I believe God feels the same internal concern.

Many times, when life takes a turn for the worse, Christians believe that God is punishing them. That He's directly scolding them for not being "good" children. Sadly, some Christians even place that guilt on the sufferer at a time when the load is already too heavy to bear. Is God's punishment a possible option when one is experiencing hardship? Yes. Does God punish His children? Yes. Hebrews 12:7–8 solidifies the answer by stating, "Endure hardship as discipline; God is treating you as his children. For what children are not disciplined by their father? If you are not disciplined—

and everyone undergoes discipline—then you are not legitimate, not true sons and daughters at all." However, Job was continually questioned by his friends if he had done something wrong to provoke God's anger, but he was considered by God to be "blameless and upright; he feared God and shunned evil" (Job 1:1). Just as Job lost everything but his life and did nothing to warrant such pain, so are many believers who suffer. God's allowance does not equal God's discipline.

I have found that in this world we are to expect suffering and difficulty. Jesus specifically warns us in John 16:33, "I have told you these things, so that in me you may have peace. In this world you will have trouble. But take heart! I have overcome the world." And although God does desire us to be happy, it's not His highest priority. His heart longs for us to be enveloped in greater riches than simple pleasure. God is sovereign and does have an ultimate cosmic plan— that story has been unfolding since the Fall of creation and is the story in which we find ourselves in the midst of now. In order for His comic plan to be fulfilled, which involves the consummation of the Kingdom of Heaven, the rescuing of souls from the bondage of sin, and current acts of redemption and restoration, He allows both good and evil to prevail. It is the age in which the "Prince of this world" is free to loot, ransack, destroy, inflict pain, torment, and attempt to overtake the "King of Kings." We're stuck in the middle of a vicious battle of spiritual principalities. And God will use us, like it or not, in His grand scheme to defeat the Enemy and restore everything fully to the way it was always meant to be. We are also subject to our own free will. God will not violate man's free will. He doesn't want puppets to obey Him, nor does He want to coerce us to love Him. He has made us to think, to choose, to create, and to be intellectually active. He limits Himself to not intervene in man's free will. Could He if He wanted to? Absolutely. He is all-powerful—but does He? No. God allows man to make His own mistakes, all the while standing in the background like a good father, interjecting His advice and direction. I believe that the pain we experience is often from wrong choices we've made or that we're possibly feeling the effects of another man's poor decisions.

I don't always know why God allows such horrendous events to transpire, but I am learning that He is trustworthy. People commonly say, "Everything happens for a reason," but I would like to disagree. Instead, I think "God brings a reason from everything that happens." He is a God of redemption and restoration. He is a God who is faithful and ultimately has our best interests in mind. He is a God who will spiritually protect even when physical protection may not happen. Often, I don't see the reason why I'm suffering when I'm suffering, but I've learned through several unanswered prayers and periods of waiting, that God actually did know what He was doing. He actually did have a better plan, one I could never have orchestrated myself. I know that I will not always see why He allows what He allows, but I think that His allowing me to have a few glimpses of the final product is His way of strengthening me for the times when the answer will never be revealed. I'm learning to trust that the heart of God is really good, and when that trust becomes more and more solidified, when I realize, despite the pain, that He's working for me and not against me, I'm able to trust that He will redeem and use for good what Satan meant for harm. "You intended to harm me, but God intended it for good to accomplish what is now being done, the saving of many lives" (Gen. 50:20).

    To the widow who mourns the death of her beloved soul mate, my heart weeps for you. To the girl whose ex-boyfriend left her wounded and shattered, my heart groans with sadness for every tear you shed. To the man who tries his best only to discover that everything he touches shatters like glass, my heart longs to grant you success a thousand times your loss. To the man who lost his job and his wife's respect, my heart wishes to fulfill your deepest needs. To the mother whose health was stolen, my heart weeps over the pain you feel, both physically and emotionally. To the cancer patient, my heart grieves with you as you hear the diagnosis and begin the treatments. To the man who lost his zeal somewhere in the midst of his job, his kids, and his emotionally distant wife, my heart desires to fix it all. To the good mother who miscarried, my heart aches to give you the child you deserve. To the loner who feels depressed and rejected, my heart longs to take you in and show you love. To the hurting, the broken, the pained, the suffering—to the ones who are abandoned and confused, alone and scared...my heart laments for all you have endured. If I of finite, limited love, yearn so deeply to heal your sorrow, how much more does the God whose identity is love and who died to rescue us from the pits of hell, long to do the same?

Chapter 14

God's Economy

How can you look at a mother who has lost her fourth child in miscarriage and with full confidence say that God is good? How can you see the boy who has struggled with cancer for many agonizing years and say that God is loving? What about an old Bible story... how can you look at the so-called "holy wars" commanded by God that resulted in mass genocide and claim, "Oh, God commanded thousands of men, woman, children, and animals to die because He is holy, just, and loving"? Pardon my frankness, but that is a God that scares the living daylights out of me and makes me want to run in the other direction. Although we established in the last chapter that God is not the cause of these atrocities, it's unsettling to know that He's still the one who permits them.

I don't understand God, His complexities, His goodness. What even is His goodness? Because I use to think His goodness comprised good things that came in good packages at very good times, not blessings in disguise. Maybe people don't always leave the church because of problems with the Christians, the so-called "hypocrites," they see. Maybe the problem is with the God that these "hypocrites" serve.

I think that it's healthy to wrestle with your faith. Paul says, "Work out your salvation with fear and trembling" (Philippians 2:12). Sometimes I wonder if I lack the fear and trembling part, but I do like the admonition to work it out. As I've mentioned previously, to be an honest Christian, you have to first and foremost be honest with yourself and God. Sometimes that honesty looks messy, "unchristian," and even blasphemous. But you have to start somewhere. What I'm thinking is not a surprise to God, so I might as well invite Him into the reflection (or, sometimes, argument). These are the dark corners of my soul that I'd rather ignore, but there is something within me that forbids me from doing so. I want to, but I can't. I have to get to the bottom of my quandary, my frustration, my fear, or reservations. I can't let it lie there and spoil like some forgotten piece of hamburger meat.

It scares me sometimes, what I find when being honest in my doubt. But I know I can't be alone. There have to be others struggling with the same question. I think in the heart of many of us is this nagging question that asks God, "Are you good? Are you *truly* good?"

Confession...at certain times in my life, I have thought God's heart to be very harsh and not good. I have then thought it to be very good indeed and, unfortunately, whiplashed back into recognizing that the core of me does not think Him to be good. But as President Clinton would say, "Define the word..." *good*.

The year my grandpa was diagnosed with lymphoma I was scheduled to be on call at the hospital for the Thanksgiving holiday. For one thing, I hate being on call—I never have liked it, probably never will—I just did it because it was a requirement and I wanted to be a team player. Secondly, Grandpa wasn't doing great but was in an uptick as far as the disease went. It was even looking like he might even be able to spend Thanksgiving Day at my parents' house and not in the nursing home, which was really exciting, especially since the doctor said he wouldn't make it to Christmas. I knew that

Thanksgiving would be the last Thanksgiving dinner we would ever have together as an entire family. I also knew that it might possibly be the last holiday ever that we would celebrate. We're a very small, very close family—so these "lasts" were big deals.

Typically, you get paged to come into the hospital when you're on call. But I also knew that God was bigger than "on call," and He could protect and preserve the family holiday somehow. He knew the desires of my heart, and those of our whole family for that matter—He knew what was best, what was prayed for, what we all were longing for. I prayed fervently for God to "preserve that day— just preserve Thanksgiving." I prayed earnestly, so that my being on call or grandpa's health wouldn't interrupt a very special, and very last, holiday. I really felt God's peace with the situation. I felt His calm—it was as if He assured me it would all be okay.

The week of Thanksgiving came. I desperately wanted the Friday after Thanksgiving off so I could spend it with family. The week before, a coworker told me that he might be available for Friday coverage. I asked him if he would cover it for me. *Suddenly* he had plans, when only a couple days prior he hadn't. I was so disappointed. I kept thinking... "If I can't get Thanksgiving off, then why can't I get the day after off? I don't think that's too much to ask. He's never there for me, and I'm always pitching in to help him." I had one last hope that one of my other coworkers would trade her Christmas Eve call for my Friday call. The next day I asked...she wouldn't. I was so beyond angry and depressed. The holiday was beginning to be a lot less fulfilling than I thought it was going to be.

The thing I wanted the most, time with family while enjoying family traditions for the last time with Grandpa, was becoming more and more unlikely.

Then Thanksgiving took another turn. Grandpa was in the ER the day before Thanksgiving with an infected bedsore. The infection was so rapid and intense that he had to immediately start IV antibiotics. His option was to be admitted to the hospital or stay at the nursing home. We chose the nursing home, which meant that his spending Thanksgiving dinner at my folks' place was completely out of the question. It was especially grieving when we knew that he'd been doing so well only three days before. When Grandpa got back to the nursing home, in his confusion he pulled out his IV. No one at the nursing home at that time was trained on how to start a new IV in his arm. If he didn't have an IV, he couldn't get his much-needed medication. I was the only one trained to reestablish the IV. So at ten p.m. that night, I started an IV (which I wasn't even sure was legal), and we ended the evening at the bedside of Grandpa, who was in a drug-induced sleep to prevent him from pulling it out again. It was really shaping up to be such a *nice* Thanksgiving.

Thanksgiving Day rolled around. I worked in the early morning but was home in time for dinner. So far, all smiles, because Grandpa's IV was still working, so he could get his antibiotics, and my other grandparents and uncle were on their way up to visit. We could still visit Grandpa at the nursing home and make the most of the day. The turkey was smelling completely amazing as always, and the family was starting to arrive. Everything was getting set on the table and right as we were getting ready to sit down and eat the delicious meal in Grandpa's absence, my phone went off. Work was calling me in. Well, that ruined it. I was so frustrated—it was all compiling. Grandpa was getting sicker, he couldn't make it to dinner, and the day I was trying to salvage and take a "positive spin on" just took an annoying turn. I could hardly taste my turkey as I shoved it angrily into my mouth before rushing off to work. I was livid! By this point, this wasn't a matter of just "bad luck." This was a fight between me and God. And boy, did I have words. I thought He was going to protect this day—keep it special—let everything work out.

I got to work clocked in, and started to get stuff ready when I received a call from the floor. They cancelled the exam that was the reason I'd been called in. What a joke! I was both happy and frustrated. I was happy that I could leave and go home to be with the family I so desperately wanted to be with and extremely ticked that my dinner and time was wasted because of a cancelled exam and an hour and twenty-minute round trip to work. I drove home, and on the way I received news that Grandpa had pulled out his IV. So instead of heading home, I headed straight to the nursing home. There was my dad, Grandpa and me—the rest of the family was at home. Perfect! Just what I hadn't prayed for—our family all scattered on our last holiday together. The nurse went to check with the head nurse if I was legally allowed to start an IV on Grandpa again. Meanwhile, Grandpa had missed two doses of his medication, and he was starting to hallucinate. It was really hard to see him in this state, but at least I was able to hold his hand and talk with him even though he wasn't making full sense. We waited on this "IV dilemma" for most of the afternoon. It took hours before they could find someone who was qualified and available to start his IV. We waited there, separated from the other half of the family, watching daylight turn into evening. By evening, the rest of the family had given up on waiting for my dad and me to return home and headed over to the nursing home. We all fit, cramped in the little nursing home room around grandpa's bed, talking, and even singing songs together while the nurses worked on Grandpa. I spent an unusual amount of time waiting with him that day—hours, in fact—waiting on the nurse, waiting on dinner, waiting, waiting, waiting. I talked a lot to him that day, and he talked quite a bit back. I held his hand a lot, too. Little did I know that would be the last conversation I would ever have with my wonderful grandpa. He passed away five agonizing days later. It still makes me want to cry. I miss him so much.

Thanksgiving was nearly everything I prayed it wouldn't be. I'd asked God to preserve the day, and I felt as though He'd told me He would. But instead, the day seemed like a total disaster. His preservation felt like His abandonment.

As I reviewed the events after Grandpa passed away, I considered God's answer to my prayers. That day was preserved in many ways, but most of the ways in which He preserved it were not the ways I had in mind. I spent the main portion of my Thanksgiving Day at my Grandpa's side—talking, singing, laughing, and holding his hand. What I wish I could do to have that back even now. I also spent time with the entire family—all of us were still together one last time on Thanksgiving. And you know what? I'm so very grateful for that. That Thanksgiving wasn't picture perfect, it wasn't free from aggravation, and it wasn't traditional or comfortable. It was hard, irritating, and upsetting, but yet somehow, it was good...very good.

Occasions like these remind us that God's definition of goodness is not really our definition of goodness. His goodness leaves many of the things we cling to very tightly up for grabs for the sake of a greater outcome, a fulfillment of the deeper desire, or the glory of His sovereignty. There is a story in the Old Testament about Elijah in the wilderness. The Lord sends an angel to prepare two cakes for him to eat. At first, when you read the story, you think, that's really cool—God provides! Then you continue to read further, and what you find out is that little did Elijah know that he wouldn't be eating anything for another forty days. The two cakes the Lord provided were to last for the next month. The story almost seems to abruptly shift from looking like God's provision to looking like God's withholding. But something that struck me odd about that story is this: Whether there is plenty or scarcity, it is still God's provision.

God's version of preservation doesn't play out the same as our view of preservation. God is eternal, immortal, infinite. He has little concern, compared to us, about the finite, mortal, and dispensable aspects of our life. By that I mean although He loves His children and does not wish for them to be harmed, He deems it of more value for them to experience such adversity so that the greater plan, blessing, and lesson will be accomplished. I do not deny that He finds even the smallest matters of yearnings, requests, and needs deeply important. However, He is far more concerned with the matters of the heart and our fidelity to Him than He is with our pleasure and comfort.

God primary goal is not to spare us from pain, shield our physical life, or work it all out before everything seems to have fallen apart; instead, His promise is to be with us through it all. If I'm being honest, I want God's top priority to be my physical safety and my happiness, so that things always have an uncanny knack to just simply work out. But over and over again in Scripture, we see a God who likes to show up right at the brink. He likes to work in the middle of impossible. We see that God values transformation and increased faith over physical rescues. God is concerned about revealing His glory in the middle of a challenging situation. He's in the business of redeeming very terrible circumstances and somehow making them good and beautiful.

Although I believe this to be true of the character of God, I often still don't like it. It grieves me, and frequently I find myself intoxicated with fear. Throughout my teen years and my adult life, I've had what I presume to be a big misperception that full surrender to God equates to ending or losing everything, like Job. I know in my head that this is a lie, but in the core of my being I struggle to say that it's untrue. Somehow I think my surrender, or lack thereof, controls how much I lose. I've believed that if I truly say, "Here I am, God. Do anything you need for Your glory," God will respond by "taking" my family, "taking" my health, "taking" my family's health...basically allowing all the most important people and things to be taken from me. And I say I believe in a *good* God?!? Slightly ironic.

I once heard a story in which a young girl was praying to God and deeply desiring to be used mightily for God's Kingdom. Months later, she was killed in a tragic accident. However, her prayers were answered. Many began to learn, to know, and to follow Jesus after her death. Frankly, that story freaks me out. But should it? If I truly believe that God is good, if I truly trust His love, then won't everything still be okay, whether in life or in death?

I don't want to lose my loved ones, and as I stared death in the face with my terminally ill grandfather, I couldn't help but be slapped by the reality that this temporal life of temporal people in temporal bodies with temporal health is passing, and continues to pass, through my fingers. I can't stop the trajectory we're on. So my theory that my complete and full surrender to God initiates and causes loss is getting debunked. Because I didn't pray that prayer before Grandpa got diagnosed with lymphoma. I didn't pray that when my mom's health began to become increasingly questionable or when my other grandpa had a second heart attack.

I'm faced, now, with some questions that need to go deeper than my intellect and register in my heart. Does my lack of surrender *prevent* loss from occurring? Does my released grip mean that all precious things *will be* taken? Is God not good even in loss? Can I control what He allows to be taken and what He gives simply by an open or closed fist? Can I add a day to my life or an hour to my day? Can I preserve the health of those I love or even my own? Is God not still good in this life or the next? Ultimately...Do I *really* trust God?

Complete surrender on all things in our life is, I believe, where God wants us. He longs for us to have that level of complete trust in Him. He wants us to recognize that His goodness goes beyond what we deem to be good. Obviously, I can't say that this is something I've conquered, but what I do know is that the people I love the most in my life (and even myself) are already aging—their health is declining. And none of that has anything to do with whether or not *I gave* God "permission" to use me however He desires for His glory. It all happened without my consent.

Psalm 84:11 says, "No good thing does he [God] withhold from those whose walk is blameless." I question this verse because good things are withheld from good people, or those I would deem "upright," God-fearing people. I've seen godly people die with cancer, god-fearing couples unable to conceive, gifted individuals taken from life at an early age...and what about Jesus? Was He not "good"? What a shameful, painful, early death! I often find myself pinched by the colliding "goods." Is my God good? Yes—He says that He is. Is my God's goodness the same as what I hope it to be? No. Is my God trustworthy? Yes—more than anybody; He is the author of trust. However, can I trust that I won't get hurt? No. Can I trust that my family won't get hurt? No. Can I trust that our health will all stay intact? No. Can I trust that the pain I go through will seem worth it to me, as it apparently is to God? No. So the real question really becomes...who or what is Lord of your life? God? Or your physical security?

These questions are so hard for me. So hard! God's character has been called into question. And as I hold on to the things that make me feel physically secure, those precious things are slipping away. I have no control, as hard as I try, to the final outcome of the things I grasp. Life takes over, sin ruins plans, and God's redemptive story does not always unfold as gloriously and painlessly as I'd hoped. However, I keep bowing to the illusive concept that yes, somehow my grasping and my release control the outcome. And so I withhold from God, who I assume is withholding from me.

God's goodness is a reflection of His character. It can seem cruel that He allows us to suffer. It can seem almost evil that holiness is protected more than woman and children. It can seem challenging that justice is just as passionately doled out as grace. To be honest, there are times when I look at who God is, learn more of His entire nature, and instead of bowing humbly at His feet, I want to run, tremble, and hide. "Who is this King of glory?" (Psalm 24:10).

And so this brings me to the real heart of the matter. God's goodness remains constant, and God's sovereign plan remains constant despite my full surrender or the lack thereof. There are two basic concepts we can deduce from this:

1. *The heinous acts, the tragedy, the joy, and the plenty are all going to happen—it's life running its course—and God extends an offer to me to surrender so that I may either have my heart prepared for the trial and/or become a participant in the blessing.*

2. *My definition of good and God's definition of good are two very different things.*

I would like to linger at the second concept for a moment. So either God is a liar, or *good* must mean something vastly different, as stated earlier. Scripture tells us in Numbers 23:19, "God is not human, that he should lie, not a human being, that he should change his mind. Does he speak and then not act? Does he promise and not fulfill?" So we know that it must be true that what God values as good is vastly different than what humans value as good.

I love John 11 because it explains this to me so well. Lazarus, the brother of Mary and Martha, is very sick, to the point of death. Mary and Martha send a message to tell Jesus that Lazarus is dying so that he might come to their aid. But the Bible tells us that Jesus first states, "This sickness will not end in death. No, it is for God's glory so that God's Son may be glorified through it." This is important because what happens later on seems to contradict this.

Directly following this verse, the story goes on to say, "Now Jesus *loved* Martha and her sister and Lazarus. So when he heard that Lazarus was sick, "*he stayed where he was two more days*, and then he said to his disciples, 'Let us go back to Judea,'" [emphasis mine]. Now, does this raise a red flag for anybody here, or is it just me? Martha and Mary are so worried about their brother dying that they cry out to the only one they know will be able to help them. And what does Jesus do? He doesn't run to their aid immediately. He doesn't come when they call. No, He waits. And it's not like He waits just to finish dinner or to pack his bags. No, He waits two days! But this is the part that catches my attention every time I read it. Just before the narrative describes how Jesus waits to visit Martha and Mary, it interjects something vitally important for us to understand.

It prefaces the wait with a small disclaimer, "Now Jesus *loved* Martha and her sister and Lazarus." He loves them, and so out of love...He waits.

Now remember that Jesus said, "this sickness will not end in death"? Later on in the passage, after a brief discourse with His disciples about returning to Judea, a city where the Jews would threaten to stone Him, He explains to the disciples how Lazarus is not sleeping due to illness but rather is dead: "so then [Jesus] told them plainly, 'Lazarus is dead, and for your sake I am glad I was not there, so that you may believe. But let us go to him.'" Again, does anybody else find this confusing? Didn't Jesus just say that this sickness will not end in death? Now He's saying that Lazarus is dead, and on top of that He's asserting that He's glad about it. Then we find out that Jesus not only waited two days to visit Lazarus—no, He waited until Lazarus was dead. Is this not a little bit hard to swallow?

But as hard as this is to comprehend, there's something very enlightening about this part of the story. Jesus states that He is glad... why? He's glad so that they might believe. There's something bigger going on besides life and death, something even more important to Jesus, something that was the sole purpose behind his waiting to visit Lazarus...and this is belief. Belief is the prize. Belief is the foundation of trust with God. Trust in God is our lifeline.

Now let's jump ahead a few verses. Jesus finally arrives in Judea to visit Lazarus and his sisters. The Bible tells us that Lazarus had been in the tomb for four days. Imagine this—this means that

Lazarus had already been wrapped and should have been starting the decay process. The reality of death had set in for both sisters. Their brother was gone. There was no turning back, no hoping he would rally from the illness. This means that they called to Jesus and instead of seeing Jesus rush to their aid, they were left feeling alone and forgotten as they watched their brother slip away. Several people had already come to comfort the sisters in the tragic loss of their brother. They were well into the grieving process.

Now if I'm being honest, if I were Martha or Mary, I would have been angry with the Lord. How could he not come when I begged for his help? But instead this is what happens, "Lord,' Martha said to Jesus, 'if you had been here, my brother would not have died. But I know that even now God will give you whatever you ask'" (John 11:21-22). We hear the angst in Martha's plea. "Where were you Jesus—I needed you! Had you come he would not have died! He wouldn't have died!" But coupled with the heartache, there is that small little seed of trust. She knows that death is not too big for Jesus to overcome. She knows that, even still, Jesus can bring life from decay. And Jesus uses this opportunity not to concentrate on the pain but rather to concentrate on His transformative, redemptive plan. He says, "I am the resurrection and the life. The one who believes in me will live, even though they die; and whoever lives by believing in me will never die. Do you believe this?" And she answers...yes. Because Jesus loved them, He was glad that they would endure this because He knew it would strengthen their belief.

Now Jesus talks with the other sister, Mary. And between her gasps and tears of anguish, she cries out to Jesus, "Lord, if you had been here, my brother would not have died." And what happens next is simply beautiful and profound. "When Jesus saw her weeping, and the Jews who had come along with her also weeping, he was deeply moved in spirit and troubled. 'Where have you laid him?' he asked. 'Come and see, Lord,' they replied. Jesus wept" (John 11:33-35).

This is the part that resonates so deeply with me. Jesus understands our pain. Jesus, the very likeness and exact representation of God, understands and feels our pain (Hebrews 1:3, Colossians 1:15). So much so that He weeps with us. He is moved within Himself and weeps with us. Do you see that? When Jesus saw Mary weeping, He was deeply moved in spirit and troubled to the point of distressing tears. The beauty of the incarnation...a God who feels, a God who understands.

Now there is more to this story, and Lazarus actually is raised to life. I know that we all don't get that same happy ending to our stories. Your husband was not brought to life, your child's cancer was not healed...but there is something very important we discover about the heart and nature of God through this passage. We see that God values trust more than the security of life itself, more than preventing heartache and pain, and more than rushing to fix the problem when we beg him to come. We see that God values opportunities to build our faith above all of these. We see that God understands that humanly, these events are ever so painful and difficult; most importantly, we see that God cares. He bears the burden with us. He enters the pain with us. And He does it all in love. Remember, "Now Jesus *loved* Martha and her sister and Lazarus. So he [waited] where he was two more days" (John 11:5-6).

God considers "good things" to be primarily spiritual in nature and not necessarily physical. We, in our temporal minds and bodies, most often equate good with physical securities—maybe God, in His eternal, infinite self, equates good things with spiritual securities. If this is true, this puts us in a unique position, because when we pray, we must recognize that the good we long for and the good we receive can't always come in the safety, comfort, and protection we find on this earth. Apparently, those physical blessings are considered more dispensable for the sake of gaining spiritual blessings. God's economy is not exchanging physical safety for temporal fulfillment, but rather His currency is that of spiritual, lasting qualities—the matters of the soul.

Truthfully, I don't really like this approach God takes to blessings. It makes me feel vulnerable, exposed, and afraid to trust Him. I want to trust that His goodness is the same as my definition of goodness all the time. I pray for spiritual growth, for certain things to be preserved or fulfilled—I pray it hoping that I will not have to endure sacrifice or pain to get there. I struggle with accepting God's goodness in the way He packages it. I want a bow and pretty paper, and He sends it with mud and stink. I want immediate gratification, and He sends instructions to assemble. I want it placed in my lap, and He makes me travel to get it.

After the Fall of mankind in the Garden of Eden, God gave us what we asked for...independence. We chose against Him personally, corporately, and as a nation. God has given this time to Satan to reign and allows the consequences of the freewill choices of man to play out. Because of that, this world can at times be a very dark place in which to live. Sometimes life is just cruel, death is too frequent, and pain feels more common than happiness. God knows this. And although in His sovereign plan He allows this, it's not His heart's desire. His heart's desire is for "all people to be saved and to come to the knowledge of the truth" (1 Timothy 2:4). So God uses this less-than-perfect world, with less-than-perfect circumstances to encourage less-than-perfect people to long for the Perfect. He wants to reveal His glory in impossible situations, transform us into the likeness of Christ, and build our faith in Him. These are the things that are important to God. These are the things that God deems very good.

And just when we begin to think He is arrogant or that He doesn't care, we realize that He, Himself, came down to experience it all with us and for us. So that when we weep over the death of a loved one, He weeps, too. So that when we hurt over the assault of an enemy, He hurts, too. We have a God who feels, and we have a God who cares.

God doesn't promise to keep us safe from all harm, but He does promise to enter into the harm with us. "When you pass through the waters, I will be with you; and when you pass through the rivers, they will not sweep over you. When you walk through the fire, you will not be burned; the flames will not set you ablaze" (Isaiah 43:2). God does not promise to make everything easy or work out how we planned but He does promise to bring beauty from the ashes. "And we know that in all things God works for the good of those who love him, who have been called according to his purpose" (Romans 8:28). God does not promise to make life easy for us, but He does promise that He will always be by our side. "I will never leave you nor forsake you. Be strong and courageous" (Joshua 1:5b, 6a).

I can't be comforted that what I have now is what I'll always have, or that I'll always be protected. With life's entropy, unpredictability, and natural trajectory, that is unfortunately a false security. But I can cling to something God impressed upon my heart many years ago: "Enjoy the moments you have right now. Things will change one day, and you don't know how, so enjoy what has been given to you." Life is fleeting, but God is faithful. His goodness will never fail.

Chapter 15

Satan and His Posse

After the fire, the problems in life seemed quite small in comparison to what could have been. Stuff didn't get under my skin too much, and the problems of life seemed to just be a small blip in heightened emotion. My perspective felt right for once...finally. I didn't stop believing that life is often cruel and that a person must be real about their raw true emotions. I didn't lose touch with the fact that not everything is buttercups and roses. I just finally felt so happy and grateful that it was enough to pull me through all other negativity. One day I was on the phone with one of my close friends, and she jokingly said, "Call me when the newness of life wears off." I laughed and said "Okay, I will. I hope it doesn't."

About two months later I called her back and left her a voicemail saying something to the effect of "Hey, it's me, and the newness of life has worn off. I'm so upset and so frustrated. Call me back because I need to vent." She called me back, and we kind of chuckled as she asked, "What's wrong?" I felt so guilty for the fact that the "newness of life" wearing off was even an option. I'd gotten so overwhelmed by everything. I felt emotionally downtrodden and explosive in anger; I felt as though life had dealt me a tough blow again. What the heck? I couldn't figure it out. What had happened? I proceeded to spend the next three months struggling with one defeat after another. *This isn't how I'm supposed to be*, I kept thinking. How had I gone from loving my life to hating it?

It took about three months for my apartment to be put back to a livable condition. Those three months weren't exactly smooth; instead, they were full of those "blessings in disguise." Because I was still in a glass half-full sort of mindset, the frustrations passed and the silver lining quickly surfaced. Finally, I moved back into my apartment after my brief sabbatical at my folk's house. I kind of had mixed sentiments. It was good to restart and to get into a normal routine again, yet a certain safety net seemed to have broken at the realization that I would have to reestablish myself in a place that didn't feel as secure. Nevertheless, I knew it was just irrational fear—it was something I had to do and could do. It would just be a little unnerving at first.

Well unnerving "at first" turned into worrying for months. Not exactly what I expected. Before I settled in and actually stayed a night at my apartment, I'd celebrated my "Alive and Twenty-five" birthday party the week before. I had a large group over and was heating up food in the new oven. (It was the first time I'd turned on an oven in that apartment since the night of the fire.) As we were all laughing, catching up, and munching, the smoke alarm suddenly went off. I panicked. The sound I wanted most not to hear ever again was piercing my ears and sending chills down to my toes. It was a trigger that immediately took me back to the fire. I promptly shut off my oven, and my friends all reassured me that there were no flames. They tried to calm me down by telling me the oven was just burning off chemicals because it was the first time it had been used. I remember shaking like a leaf—just quivering—over something so insignificant.

The next week I had enough moved in to actually begin sleeping there. Food, clothes, toiletries...everything was there and ready for me to commence residency. I'm sure that, for a guy, all that would be needed is a frozen pizza and a pillow, but of course, me being a girl and all, it was essential that not only my hair straightener was there but also my shoes and jewelry. I called in my best friend to "babysit" me and stay a couple nights. I used to be fine living on my own, but now, suddenly, it didn't feel as harmless—it felt foreign. I spent the first three weeks alone at night in a near state of paralysis. I kept thinking I heard someone coming up the steps or breaking through the door. Fear had consumed me. I felt like I was on guard all night to defend my house and myself. I was extremely tired from not being able to sleep at night. I once called my parents in the wee hours of the morning and swore that I heard my washing machine running in my basement without having turned it on. When I finally mustered up enough nerve to walk downstairs, I sheepishly discovered that it had been off the whole time.

More sleepless nights followed as my fear seemed to subside, only to be replaced by emotional drama. My singleness, which I'd been content and at peace with only weeks before, suddenly seemed unbearable and unfair. Soon old emotions from an old relationship resurfaced, which sent me spiraling into a whirlwind of self-depreciation. I began bashing who I was and how "stupid" I was for feeling this way. Every small thing was heightened with unnecessary emotion, whether it was anxiety, sadness, or irritations. I wasn't myself. Meanwhile, work became unusually challenging. My future, which just months earlier had looked so bright and promising, seemed to quickly turn bleak, and I wasn't even quite sure why.

I began to realize that I was being spiritually attacked by the Enemy. I always hate to give the devil and his crew too much credit, but when the accusations became overbearing, I began to uncover that this was more than a bad day or a bad month, or even a bad couple of months; it was an attack in which the Enemy was trying to knock me down. I would cry myself to sleep, you know, the "ugly cry," as I begged God for help. I would either lie in my bed or kneel on the floor, pleading with God for peace because I knew I couldn't keep living life this way. Somehow, I had allowed the devil a foothold into my emotional well-being. If you've ever struggled with anxiety or depression, you may be able to relate to this. I felt accusation after accusation pummel me, and I felt unable to defend myself. I called out to God to shield me, to fight off the mental and emotional invasions, but the war kept on. I began beating myself up more. So then my tears were not only shed for frustrations over emotions but poured out from a cavernous pit of self-loathing. In my mind I could not understand how God could possibly love me. I knew the depth of my sin, and I knew that the way I was, was not at all who He wanted me to be. I particularly remember one lonely, senseless sob-session. Hugging my tissue box, I laid in my bed as if sick in the hospital, staring out into my dark bedroom and hearing loudly and clearly (not audibly but in my heart), "You look ugly when you cry. You look so ugly. God even thinks you look ugly. How could God *not* think you look ugly?" I know people joke about the "ugly cry" but I remember knowing in my head that this was not a joke— these were accusations. These were in no way words from God but that night, all I could feel was God seeing my ugliness and declaring it to me as I wept and thrashed my head at the very real belief that my ugliness was detestable to God. After that night, I really was convinced that the Enemy was at work. I had watched one attack merge into another sort of attack which merged into another type of attack. He was relentless, and I lost my footing each time his wave of accusations washed over me. It felt impossible to come up for air. I didn't know how to fight back.

One lonely Friday night, after the sun set, as well as my heart...to the depths of depression that it had grown so accustomed to, I decided to take out a purple magic marker and a rather large piece of paper, a 3- by 2 ½-foot piece from the white backside of wrapping paper. I cleared off the side of my refrigerator that was exposed, taped and magnet-posted the blank slab on the side of the fridge. On the top I wrote "Lies, Things I Hate About Myself." I proceeded to take the next one to two hours to write down every accusation I had been hearing, carrying around, hating, and feeling so assuredly during my life, especially from the previous month. My white backdrop quickly turned purple. I ran out of room. One thing after another, after another...on and on. One accusation connected with another lie, which resonated with another half-truth. I'd start to put the cap on the marker, and again I'd remember something else and then another thing. I remember taking my chair from the dining room table and setting it in the hall directly in front of my loaded paper. I sat down and starred at my splattered markings and with reserved astonishment, I thought, *Wow, no wonder I've felt as awful as I have lately.* I had been carrying this all around, every day, every night, through every good and bad experience. I was drowning in self-hatred and not quite sure which way was up. I sat there a little longer and with a mixture of sadness and emptiness stated, "Now what, God?"

I realized during those months that I wanted a God who could handle my humanity because it felt like no one else could. I wasn't convinced that God could handle me, either. The hardest parts of those months were not the trials at work or the emotional baggage; it was the fact that my faith became more of a problem and an area of confusion than help for me. I felt incredibly loaded down with guilt and daily felt God's frown and disappointment on my personhood.

It took a while to first figure out what was going on and second, to figure out how to fix it. I talked to a lady with whom I'd been going through a Christian devotional and told her that I felt as if my life were passing me by and that I was feeling so unhappy. I said how I felt as though I'd been relentlessly attacked since I moved back into my place. She said, "Maybe you were really starting to grasp some truths after your fire; maybe that's why you're under attack." I think she hit the nail on the head. The Enemy saw the start of a good thing and came in for the kill to overpower the truths with his lies.

I really hate to give the weaselly devil credit—it's like calling a dog, and his ears perk up. However, it's necessary to recognize that being a Christian does not keep you immune from the Enemy. In fact, I believe the devil will hone in harder on those who are trying to truly press into God. He will do everything in his power to weaken your efforts to grow in Christ. To believe he isn't at work is an unwise stance to take because ignoring his activity puts you in a defenseless position, which can potentially be detrimental. The months of struggle really came as a surprise to me. I felt a little blindsided, and I guess that is all part of the tactic. Pick on an unsuspecting soul—and it totally worked. He got me! I spent a few weeks coming to the realization that I was in a battle, but then came the hard work...how do I fix it?

There's a line in a Dave Matthews song in which the girl in the story is in a miserable state of life. She asks herself, *Am I supposed to take in on myself to get out of this place?*[22] That's how I felt. I'd been pleading with God over the past few months to only feel His distance and displeasure. So when the God of the universe seems to be MIA, I guess it's time to do something yourself, right? But what? The only thing I had particularly mastered was crying myself to sleep and complaining a lot. Obviously, that wasn't working.

This is where addictions are bred. I heard someone say one time, "If you feel dirty, you act dirty."[23] It's true, if you feel you've already messed up your life, asked for God's wrath, and sold your soul to the devil, then taking on another "sin" really is no big deal. You might as well have fun if you have already deemed yourself as being unworthy. So people start turning to porn, alcohol, drugs, sex, food...something...anything to give a second of reprieve and put a smile back on the face. This is exactly where the opposing team wants you—at this point the devil thinks he is winning. Because now you not only have the original depression, but you also have a side of failure with a complimentary dish of addiction topped off with a dessert of self-hatred. Therein lies some unwanted calories!

For those of us who claim to believe in this guy who's called Jesus and who walked on water, this threshold of depression and addiction is a pivotal point at which we can walk or sink. I've been walking (or maybe sinking) with Jesus for quite some time now, and I'm just now starting to realize that I don't have to sink any longer. During month two of the "I hate my life phase," I met with an old friend. He's a pastor now, but we've known each other since 8th grade. He asked me about life. I don't really hide my emotions too well, so whether or not he wanted to hear my true feelings about life, I told him, and he listened. I said, "I don't know what else to try. I've tried everything." And like any good pastor, he challenged me to read my Bible more consistently...and like any bratty child, I pulled the "I don't wanna" card. I told him all my reservations, and the frustrations that came with reading that ancient book. It's not that I didn't read it from time to time, but every time I read it, it seemed particularly difficult. I believed in its power but didn't know how or when that power would work for me. I tried to reason with him that I spent a lot of time in prayer and in reading Christian books, but the Bible is challenging for me. I explained how it makes me feel "condemned" or even more like a failure. Instead of feeling peace and freedom, I seemed to feel more like a jerk because I'm just not that perfect Christian I know I should be—you know, the one who isn't supposed to complain or frown, or eat junk food. He gave me a forty-day challenge to read my Bible every day. I gave him a few sighs and an eye roll and begrudgingly agreed. He offered to be available for any questions, and I frequently took him up on his offer.

I can't say that the forty days were life-changing. I didn't fall in love with the Bible or hear angels singing. I did it because I made a commitment and because I knew it was right. I also felt pretty hopeless and needed something, because I was convinced it was not God's will for me to live a life overrun with depression and self-hatred. I didn't stop reading other Christian books, and I definitely didn't stop praying. Slowly, it began to sink in that all these truths I was reading mattered and that they were applicable to my life and to my predicament. I had the power at my fingertips, but I was standing in the crossfire and, like a pacifist, was refusing to shoot. I had authority given to me but was acting like a civilian when I was royalty. I don't think I'd forgotten who I was in Christ; I think I had just finally started to uncover what it actually meant.

Here's what I found...there is truth, absolute truth, that *must* be claimed—not thought about, not considered, not read...but claimed over your life. When you choose to follow Jesus and model His life, you've just made yourself a target for the Enemy. He doesn't care if you're blind to Jesus, if you're an atheist, or if you're just a moral person doing moral things with no substance of belief. He's happy, because then you're on his side, and the best part is, you don't even know it. But when the blinders come off and your eyes are opened to this Jesus fellow, the Enemy begins to fret. He's about to lose a team player, and he will start crafting a way to win you back. Then, if you fully commit to this arch-nemesis of his, he will try to make you lose any battle he possibly can. The devil's no dummy. He knows your areas of weakness, so he will cater specifically to those until you start losing every battle. Utterly defeated, you willing resign yourself to an "unworthy," "useless" status, or, better yet, you become very comfortable with apathy, both options that give Satan great joy. He may have lost a teammate, but he's wounded you badly enough that you are out of the game.

The word *gospel* means "good news." Frankly, there have been times when I've scratched my head and said, "Huh, good news? How?" I think the problem begins when you've taken a good look at yourself and realize how dissatisfied you are with who you are and how you act. From your self-survey, you can only conclude that God must also dislike you. Then you have piles of accusations that say, "You aren't good enough," "You suck at life," "You're a failure," "There you go, you screwed up again," spoken to you from the opposing team. Maybe that doesn't describe you. You may not reside in the self-depravity camp. You may find yourself in the opposite arena, believing that you are good enough. You think, "I'm not that bad, especially not as bad as the church wants to make me sound." You compare yourself to others and see how successful, kind, and good you really are. And the proof is in the pudding—you're a respectable citizen, you don't lie, you are top-notch at your job, a loving parent and spouse...you're not a bad person. Although you're convinced that Jesus had a purpose and did in fact make a sacrifice, you believe that it's not something to lose your head over. Despite natural defenses saying otherwise, this is another set of lies and blinders the Enemy uses that cause us to rationalize our stink and keep Jesus at arm's length. We begin to absorb those lies as truths—our justified worldview. Then as we believe them, we live them out as a conviction, as if they define our lives. The good news doesn't seem that good, because we believe that we're either too good or too awful to see it for what it's worth. But here is some very good news: We have every right—and every ability—to not be defined by these misunderstandings.

When individuals commit their lives to Jesus, they receive the forgiveness that has *already been* given. God can't handle sin and, in all reality, the parts we hate (and sometimes love) about ourselves would be detestable to Him because His perfection couldn't handle it. But God can't help Himself...for some reason, He loves us, because His very identity is love. He loves His creation, all of it, but even more so, He loves His crowned creation: us. So to live without us is upsetting to Him. It's not what He wants, and it's not how it was intended to be, so He made a way to satisfy His identity as a judge and His identity as a lover. Something had to appease His wrath, to make up for all the damage we've done. But a mess doesn't fix a mess. Perfection fixes a mess, and so God made a way to be with us through Jesus, the epitome of perfection. When Christ died, God's wrath, and the judgment needed to sentence us, was instead cast on Christ so that we would be spared the penalty. As we all know—even those of us who don't claim to be Christians—Christ died but did not stay dead. He conquered death and was resurrected.

Let me take a very brief moment, here, to apologize for a possible "preachy presentation"; however, I can't apologize for the message. This story is the crux of the matter, and the story must be repeated. We must start at the beginning to realize why the ending is so important, why the good news is truly good news. This story, in America, has been rehearsed as often as the fairy tale of "Snow White and the Seven Dwarfs." Unfortunately, I think that it's commonplace to equate the two stories and to parallel historical facts with the credibility of childhood tales. This is where I'm going to ask you to pause, so I can deduce some very important conclusions from the familiar story involving Jesus, a tree, and an empty tomb.

Jesus did not stay dead. Now this chapter is not here to lay out the facts and archeological findings of how we know for sure that Jesus didn't stay dead (you can find more helpful resources in the back of this book to help you dig deeper on this topic). It's a historical fact, and for the sake of staying on topic, I will leave you to do your own research if you doubt it. (I am assured that you'll come to the same conclusion, and if you think otherwise—I dare you to prove me wrong.) The fact that Jesus conquered death is key. Jesus conquering death means He conquered the ruler of death and the powers of death, Satan and his posse. This means that the war has already been won. PAST TENSE—already done, finished, accomplished, complete, finito...done! But what I've found to be true in my own life and in the lives of many Jesus followers is that we live as if this all hasn't happened. Of course, this may not apply to everybody, but many of us live as if we're unforgiven. We live as if God views us as miserable, hopeless, screwed-up sinners. We live as if we must pay penance for our wrongdoings—hoping our penance will earn us enough "good points" so that God will show us favor. When we read the promises or truths of the Bible, we live as if they lack application in our lives and applied only to the Romans, to the Corinthians, or to any of the other folks back then. We forgo our right to claim the promises *now*. The Bible transcends time because its Author transcends time. And although you must understand a verse in its original context—you can extrapolate the transcending truths that were applicable then, now, and to the children of our children's children.

I believe that God, like a good coach, doesn't want His team to be defeated. So He instills truths about who the players are, what their potential is, what He expects, and methods for defeating the opposing team. The Bible, in a sense, is God's coaching manual. God chooses not to play for His players because His goal is not to do everything for His team. Rather, His goal is to empower them to play how He knows they can play. That's why I sometimes think that we feel alone in the attack. We stand defenseless, expecting the coach to fight for us when it's our turn to take what we've learned and put it into practice. God knows our potential for evil, and He knows our potential for good, but He has placed great confidence in us to overcome evil with good. God is not a "kick 'em when they're down" coach. He's the coach that says, "I believe in you. You can do it. Go do what you were meant to do."

Something clicked, one week, while I was learning about the opposing team. I finally saw the intimidation and lies Satan uses to attempt to devalue our personhood or to superficially puff us up. He's all bark and no bite. Satan has no more power over you than what you afford him. If you're under the covering of Christ, your position before God can't be taken. If you ever want to stop yielding your life to the Enemy, you have to begin to give him less ground and less ego. Coach tells us to take every thought captive: "We demolish arguments and every pretension that sets itself up against the knowledge of God, and we take captive every thought to make it obedient to Christ" (2 Cor. 10:5). Coach also says we need to renew our minds so we can figure out how to defeat the tactics used against us. "Do not conform any longer to the pattern of this world, but be transformed by the renewing of your mind. Then you will be able to test and approve what God's will is--his good, pleasing and perfect will" (Romans 12:2). Notice how Coach emphasizes the power of the mind? That's where the cosmic game begins—in the field of thoughts. This is where the Opposing Team gets to us, highlights our failures, overemphasizes our successes, condemns our actions, bloats our self-esteem, insults our person, blinds our immorality, and creates a keen awareness of our very real unworthiness (or independence) to God. "For our struggle is not against flesh and blood, but against the rulers, against the authorities, against the powers of this dark world and against the spiritual forces of evil in the heavenly realms" (Ephesians 6:12).

So all that to say, here's the really "good news"...our unworthiness does not change God's faithfulness. Because of the story of Jesus, with its cross and empty tomb, God sees us with a new pair of spectacles. We, who humble ourselves enough to choose to receive the covering of the work done by Christ, are seen by God as if we are Christ. We are sons and daughters now. We're not outside the door, like random strangers; we're in the family. "Consequently, you are no longer foreigners and aliens, but fellow citizens with God's people and members of God's household" (Ephesians 2:19). Now that is good news! God does not see us as vessels damned to destruction; He sees us as covered and forgiven by the cleansing sacrifice of Christ. "You are all sons of God *through faith in Christ Jesus*, for all of you who were baptized into Christ have clothed yourselves with Christ" (Galatians 3:26). We are simultaneously sinners and forgiven. So although we sin, we aren't subject to the power that sin has over the world—the death-giving power of sin has already been conquered.

The beautiful reality is that my lack of feeling peace with God doesn't mean that it still hasn't already been accomplished. "He was delivered over to death for our sins and was raised to life for our justification. Therefore, since we have been justified through faith, we have peace with God through our Lord Jesus Christ, through whom we have gained access by faith into this grace in which we now stand" (Rom 4:45–5:2). My belief that God is displeased doesn't make God displeased. My belief that God is pleased with me also doesn't make Him pleased with me. God is who He is because His character is unchanging. It's not about me. What I do or don't do doesn't affect what work has already been done through Jesus' sacrifice. The work has been accomplished. Forgiveness has been offered. Peace has been given. Hope still abounds. Love, mercy, and grace are freely bestowed. Favor is already extended. Reconciliation has already been made. This is the Good News for those who choose to accept it. This is the power that we are all privy to if we choose to tap into it. This is the authority that covers us if we choose to step under it. You can live defeated, and you can ignore these truths. You can let your pride tell you that you're better than you really are. You can choose to reject the whole notion and chalk Jesus up to a fairy tale. You have every right to do so. You're not obligated, by any means, to accept this as applicable to your life. Neither should you feel coerced into something you don't want to believe. You need to choose for yourself what you think is right. However, the offer is still there; it always will be there. It's really not about you. The God of the universe has already done a great work and reconciled the world to Himself. It's totally up to you to accept or reject the inheritance.

I believe that God's desire is for all of us to choose to accept what's been done and to live a fulfilling life. I'm convinced that for those of us who have accepted the gifts already given and have committed to live the "Christian life," we're not meant to live the life defeated, scared, and half-present. We're to live fully awake, through pain and pleasure. And we are to live with our heads up, eyes engaged, feet ready, shoulders back, and heart abandoned as we run toward the embodiment of love, Jesus Christ (Phil 3:13b). Coach tells us to be filled with the Spirit (Ephesians 5:18), unfettered to the lies that claw at us. Why live as victims, when we are the victors? Satan has already met his match—he just tries ferociously to prove otherwise. Your best defense is to remember that your identity was founded in the Victor's grace. So let me tell you who you are, and may you claim these truths over your heart and mind:

You are a child of God, a son, a daughter...an heir to the gifts already given. "So you are no longer a slave but a son; and since you are a son, God has made you also an heir" (Galatians 4:7). "For you did not receive a spirit that make you a slave again to fear, but you received the Spirit of sonship" (Romans 8:15). "The Spirit himself testifies with our spirit that we are God's children" (Romans 8:17).

You are seen by God as if you were Christ. He doesn't see your filth and hold it against you. He sees you with the same love, admiration, and acceptance that He has for His son, Jesus. "For you died, and your life is now hidden with Christ in God. When Christ, who is your life, appears, then you also will appear with him in glory" (Colossians 3:1–4).

You are a work of art, God's handiwork, a masterpiece. "For we are God's workmanship" (Ephesians 2:10).

You have the mind of Christ because you have received the Holy Spirit. "We have not received the Spirit of the world but the Spirit who is from God… but we have the mind of Christ" (1 Corinthians 2:12 and 16).

You are submersed in God's love. You can't escape it even if you wanted to. "For I am convinced that neither death nor life, neither angels nor demons, neither the present nor the future, nor any powers, neither height nor depth, nor anything else in all creation, will be able to separate us from the love of God that is in Christ Jesus our Lord" (Romans 8:38–40).

You are set free from the power of sin. You don't have to let it conquer you, because you have the power to conquer it. "But thanks be to God that, though you used to be slaves to sin, you wholeheartedly obeyed the form of teaching to which you were entrusted. You have been set free from sin, and have become slaves to righteousness" (Romans 6:17–18).

You are considered worthy, not because of what you have done, but because Jesus covers you with His blood. God "gives life to the dead and calls things that are not as though they were" (Romans 4:18).

You have purpose. You are meant to do good things, and there is much work to be done. "For we are God's workmanship, created in Christ Jesus to do good works, which God prepared in advance for us to do" (Ephesians 2:10).

You are noticed and heard by God. "The LORD will hear when I call to him" (Psalm 4:3).

You need not worry about man's power. You need to answer to God. You are not a "yes-man," always bowing to everyone else's requests to meet their approval. You need only be concerned with God's approval. "I care very little if I am judged by you or by any human court; indeed, I do not even judge myself. My conscience is clear, but that does not make me innocent. It is the Lord who judges me" (1 Corinthians 4:3–4).

You have been given a spirit of power, love, and self-discipline. "For God did not give a spirit of timidity, but a spirit of power, of love and of self-discipline" (2 Timothy 1:7).

You are "worth it" to God. He will not give up on the good work He has started in you. He *will* complete it—not "He

'might,'" but "He 'will.'" "He who began a good work in you will carry it on to completion until the day of Christ Jesus" (Philippians 1:6).

You have Jesus constantly interceding on your behalf when accusations are brought against you. When Satan tells God that you've fallen, that you've failed in many areas, and that you've offended Him, Jesus quickly covers you and says that He knows you, you are His, and you have been forgiven, are being forgiven, and will always be forgiven. "Therefore he is able to save completely those who come to God through him, because he always lives to intercede for them. Such a high priest meets our need—one who is holy, blameless, pure, set apart from sinners, exalted above the heavens. Unlike the other high priests, he does not need to offer sacrifices day after day, first for his own sins, and then for the sins of the people. He sacrificed for their sins once for all when he offered himself. For the law appoints as high priests men who are weak; but the oath, which came after the law, appointed the Son, who has been made perfect forever" (Hebrews 7:25–28).

You can come to God confidently and boldly because of what Jesus did. "Therefore, since we have a great high priest who has gone through the heavens, Jesus the Son of God, let us hold firmly to the faith we profess. For we do not have a high priest who is unable to sympathize with our weaknesses, but we have one who has been tempted in every way, just as we are—yet was without sin. Let us then approach the throne of grace with confidence, so that we may receive mercy and find grace to help us in our time of need" (Hebrews 4:14–16).

You are forgiven. Your sins are put behind you. You are

seen as forgiven by God. "You see, at just the right time, when we were still powerless, Christ died for the ungodly. Very rarely will anyone die for a righteous man, though for a good man someone might possibly dare to die. But God demonstrates his own love for us in this: While we were still sinners, Christ died for us. Since we have now been justified by his blood, how much more shall we be saved from God's wrath through him! For if, when we were God's enemies, we were reconciled to him through the death of his Son, how much more, having been reconciled, shall we be saved through his life! Not only is this so, but we also rejoice in God through our Lord Jesus Christ, through whom we have now received reconciliation" (Romans 5:6-11).

I wrote myself a reminder, in my own words, of how God views me. So when the time comes when either I can't stand myself or someone else can't, I can go to this. Let me leave you with this benediction:

You are my child, and with You I am well pleased. Not because of the work you have done but because of My namesake. You have been redeemed, even the ugly parts. Even the parts you hate about yourself. The work has already been done. I did not need to, no—I even should not have—for who you were was something My perfection and purity could not handle. But something about you, something about who you truly are, who you were always meant to be, how You and I were always meant to be, beckoned My compassion. We, the Trinitarian God, wanted communion with you. Why? Because you were created out of Our love, out of Our laughter, out of Our image to be known, to be loved, and to be in communion with Us. What Satan meant for harm,

We turned into good. After your Fall and your sin, and even after your failures now...you, My child, have been redeemed. You, My friend, have been reclaimed. You, My beloved, have been and will always be covered by the blood of Christ. I am Yours to have, to hold, to find shelter in. And you are Mine. I know you, all of you, for better or for worse, and I have chosen to always love you without any conditions applied. Confess to Me daily, put on My cloak of forgiveness, and live like you are loved and valued. Because you are, not for your namesake but for My namesake. I have redeemed you to live purposefully, intentionally, and beautifully. There is much work to do, My child. Go, live in My favor, which I have so freely bestowed.

Chapter 16

Everything is a Plus

Somewhere along the way, I forgot that this life is not all about me. Sometimes, I have an ugly flair-up of Only Child Syndrome (coined by my parents). I'm an only child and an only grandchild on both sides—it explains a lot! Struggle as I might, the world doesn't revolve around me. Unfortunately, I tend to forget this often, especially in the midst of what I consider to be a "mini-crisis." Like the "crisis" you have when you get a bill in the mail you weren't expecting. Or the "crisis" when, for the fourth time, this person says they'll call you back to answer your inquiry and, once again, *you* are calling *them* to follow up as if you had nothing else better to do than call repeatedly for a simple answer. I'm a big fan of the "I just got pulled over for speeding" crisis. This usually happens when you're already running late to work for the third time that week, your dog just died, or you paid $500 for auto repairs the weekend before. Or how about when your computer erases pages—not sentences—of material you just wrote because, oops, it had an error and you just happened to forget to hit save! Really?? These are the moments where we grumble and complain. Things seem unfair, and even if they are fair, they are absolutely, all-together annoying. These are times when I have caught myself thinking, "If there was a time-clock in life, I would have punched out several times by now."

I don't understand it, really. Why does life have to have so many minor obstacles? Because we all know there is an overabundance of major obstacles. I continually make the mistake of assuming that something is going to be easy. That something will just work smoothly. Who gave me that bright idea? I have no clue, because life isn't really like that. There will always be small annoyances, "impeccable" timing (note the sarcasm), and, sometimes, just plain idiots that you have to deal with. Sorry to be harsh, but it's true. We've all been there. It's natural to have knee-jerk responses to these trivial aggravations. The reaction seems so justified, so rational... the understood response to an unexpected outcome. Frustrating experiences warrant poor responses, right? But I know that this is just self-supported vindication to excuse unfitting behavior. I'm not saying that we can't respond "humanly" because, honestly, with some things, there seems to be no other option. I'm a firm believer that if you keep trying to brush it under the rug, put on the "positive Polly" smile, and continue on as if nothing has stunted your day, then soon things will build up. After time, instead of a mild release of frustration, there is a massive volcanic eruption of rage. So frustrations do need to be expressed and not just ignored.

I would argue that the core of these frustrating, anger-filled emotions is this belief that we're entitled to something more, something better. Entitlement is when we believe we deserve certain rights or privileges that we don't necessary deserve. Before my fire, that word was lying heavily on my heart. I could recognize it rooted in most all of my negative responses to small, frustrating life experiences. That's kind of where the word stayed...at the point of recognition. I didn't know what to do with the fact that I struggled with the ugly vice of entitlement. Here I was, responding like a spoiled brat to situations because I had this core belief that I'm entitled to a better, smoother, efficient, more sensible, easier, and more pleasant outcome. I remember talking with one of my friends.

I think that after talking with her, it hit me that I had to be honest with myself about the reality that I had succumbed to entitlement. My friend and I were comparing and contrasting how we respond in different situations. Although my friend wouldn't deny that life is vicious at times and very commonly unfair, she just takes it as it comes instead of fighting it. I remember her saying something to the effect that even if she were to lose her job, she would still have her family and friends, and a house to live in. But even if she lost her house, she would still have family and friends. Even if she lost her family, she would still have her friends, and even if she lost her friends, she would still have her education. The point was that to her, everything was more than what she should have ever had to begin with. You see, my friend, as an infant, was adopted from South Korea by her parents from America. They had prayed for her, and so had others in the church. Thankfully, the doors were opened, and God made a way for this little Asian girl to be adopted into a stable, loving, Christ-centered home. My friend is very aware that what she has is not what she deserves or should have had. Her life could have easily been one in an orphanage—where she didn't have a family, a house, or an education. So to her, when things go wrong, it's not the end of the world, because things could have—and should have—been a lot worse for her, and they aren't. I remember talking to her that day and realizing, *She gets it.* She understands that everything is a plus. And I? I don't.

Months later, following that conversation, I had my fire. I stood on the snowy sidewalk, staring into the black night sky with a keen awareness that I might have possibly just lost everything I owned except for the few items that I'd left at my parents' house. And in that moment, I was more convinced than not that I'd lost it all because I knew how fast the fire had taken over my kitchen and hallway in a minute's time. I was grieved that I had gone from having everything to having nothing. But I was also thankful, because in the same sense, I still had everything. I had my life, I had my God, I had my family, and I had my health.

When the smoke cleared from not only my house but from my head, I finally realized what my friend had been talking about. I was more than shocked to see that most items had made it through the fire unscathed, not to mention myself. Here I was, convinced that every belonging I owned had been torched only to discover that I still possessed them. And although, it holds no comparison to my health and life, I was so happy and so amazed that simple things—like my favorite shoes, my pretty necklaces, sentimental pictures, favorite books, shirts, and sweaters—were still mine to keep. Truly these items didn't matter compared to life, faith, health, and family, but their survival still brought me such gratitude, because I had them when I was very aware that I should not. Not only did I have the essentials, I had the extras. I realized that everything is a plus.

After a few months passed following my fire, entitlement found its way back into my heart. For a few weeks immediately after the fire, I got it. I knew what it meant that everything I owned was really extra; my belongings were not entitled to me. But then, with the pressure of fire expenses, living costs, and general discouragement at how "easy" things *weren't*, I found myself once again slipping into the traps of entitlement. I was out to dinner with a friend I hadn't seen in a while. We were discussing the frustrations of failed expectations, thwarted life timelines, and general daily challenges. As I was sitting there in the booth, complaining about unfulfilled personal longings, I ended my thought by saying aloud, "I guess life really isn't about me." Then it hit me: This life that God has granted me isn't just for me to live, so that I can be happy and do what I want when I want. The purpose of a life, even more so, the purpose of a "Christian" life, is to bring glory to God and to know Him intimately. It's not about furthering our kingdom, it's about furthering His Kingdom. This isn't new news to me, but it's news with which I seem to have a case of early-onset dementia: I remember it for a bit, and soon it gets pushed to the recesses of my memory as the complications of life pervade. If life is really not about me, then why do I fight so hard for my happiness? Strive so much for my own security? Tantrum when things aren't easy? Cry when something or someone falls through? Resist so adamantly when I don't want to do something? Life isn't about me, nor is it really all about others. Truly, life is about the its Creator...life is about being used *for* Him and *by* Him so that we may *know* Him and be *changed* by Him, hoping that eventually others may do the same.

Even if I have nothing, I have everything—right? In the heart of that phrase, there's truth. But in the heart of me, I struggle with that concept. I believe it, but when I count the cost, I internally shudder. My actions are my barometer. If I truly believed that even if I have nothing, I still possess everything, then "mini-crises" wouldn't be crises at all. And things not being easy would be an expected part of life because, after all, life wouldn't be about my happiness or even the lack thereof. If I ever wonder if that truthful statement has carved its way into my core, I need to look no further than my responses to the many challenges life doles out.

I'm not here to satisfy me. I'm a vessel that is meant to be poured out. That reality is honestly scary, because it means that I'm dispensable. If the goal, purpose, and ambition of my life is to be used as a tool by God to a lost world, then should I not yield everything I have and everything I am to be used by God as He so pleases? That takes incredible trust. That is the ultimate sacrifice, because those who commit themselves to God in such a manner tell Him that their health, their financial security, their families, their jobs, their material possessions, even their pets, their desires, and dreams are all free for the taking if that would somehow bring Him glory. Some people die an early death—not that I believe God caused their deaths, but possibly He allowed their deaths to make more of an impact in the souls of others than through their lives. God does not waste. He uses all things, both broken and intact, to project His divine love and grace to the lost world. However, it's scary to know that He may allow intact things to become broken so that His will and Kingdom plans can come to fruition.

If we want to live that way, a way of self-sacrifice and complete surrender to God, then that is most honorable. If we don't, then, frankly, it is our loss. We grasp and grasp so tightly that we lose the very thing we're grasping. It's like a mother who is trying to protect her child. She lies over the child to protect it from external dangers, but in her efforts to save the child, she smothers it to death. We hold on so tightly that we break the very life that was given us. In fear of losing it, we forsake how it was actually meant to be lived in the first place.

A passage in Luke 12 recounts the parable of the rich fool. And the more I think about it, the more I recognize that it could very well be a parable about America. Jesus speaks to a crowd:

Then he said to them, "Watch out! Be on your guard against all kinds of greed; life does not consist in an abundance of possessions." And he told them this parable: "The ground of a certain rich man yielded an abundant harvest. He thought to himself, 'What shall I do? I have no place to store my crops.' Then he said, 'This is what I'll do. I will tear down my barns and build bigger ones, and there I will store my surplus grain. And I'll say to myself, "You have plenty of grain laid up for many years. Take life easy; eat, drink and be merry."' But God said to him, 'You fool! This very night your life will be demanded from you. Then who will get what you have prepared for yourself?' This is how it will be with whoever stores up things for themselves but is not rich toward God."

We Americans have so much. We're so rich. Even those of us who could be considered poor have our basic needs, food, clothing, and shelter. We haven't been blessed with much only so that we can enjoy much and save much. We've been blessed so that we can give. We've been filled up so that we can be poured out. That's the heart of it all.

In American Christianity, we have a faith that doesn't require much of us. Yes, we can get some flack in the workplace. Yes, we don't always fit in. And more and more in the news it's evident that Christian rights are not subject to the same objectivity and non-biased views granted to other religions. But many of us don't honestly have a clue what persecution for Jesus looks like. Thankfully, we've been greatly spared from many of those atrocious experiences. Many of us don't know what it means to live by faith, where our next meal is dependent on God's direct provision. We don't know what it means to sacrifice. I've heard of believers who are so desperate for the truth of Jesus that they've walked miles just to hear the preacher—and they weren't wearing Nike Air's—they walked a dirt path in their bare feet. Then they sat on a narrow wooden bench (not a cushioned supportive chair or pew) and listened for hours (not a thirty-minute tribute) to someone talk about Jesus.

I read a book called *Revolution in World Missions*, by K. P. Yohannan. The book is profound, and if you are in need of a good read, I highly recommend this one. It's so humbling and so gripping to hear about the poverty in which much of the world lives. K.P. is a missionary who was born and raised in India and became an evangelist in his home country until he moved to America for seminary training. He compares the vast difference between the affluence of America to the poverty of India. Those of us who live in America have so much more than we even realize and much more than we need. While K. P. didn't get his first pair of shoes until he was 17 years old, we spend without hesitation on vases and wallpaper just to make our houses look more stylish.

My husband gave me one of the best Christmas gifts I could ask for—he surprised me with a mission trip to Haiti. I know that a lot of people may not view that as a great gift, but to me, it was literally an answer to prayer. I wanted to experience a mission trip with my husband—knowing that God would use it to grow us as a couple and to grow closer to Him. The trip to Haiti proved to be remarkable. As we flew into the country, we could see the miles of brown, muddy land bearing the scars of scarcity. We had a two to three hour bus ride from the airport to the compound in which we stayed. To say that the ride was eye-opening is an understatement. We saw evidence of poverty and filth that we'd never seen before. Smells of burning trash, putrefied compost, and car exhaust cycled in and out of the open-air bus. This was the Haitians' country. This was their big city...their life.

We spent almost two weeks in Grand Goave, Haiti. The people there own very little. In this country, we probably have more possessions and more protection with a simple pop-up tent on a camping trip than many of the Haitians have in their homes. Even the chickens, cows, and goats were skinny, because there is such a shortage of food. There aren't really hospitals there—their hospitals are similar to our American urgent-care clinics. People die early deaths from tuberculosis (TB), fever, and infection—all very treatable here in the States. Much of their days were spent surviving—vending in their marketplace, finding food, working jobs for no pay in order to get noticed for future potential employment—just trying to make a way.

The trip was coordinated through Lifeline Christian Mission. It's a great organization that I would highly recommend if you're looking to get involved. Among other things, Lifeline had an orphanage and school which pour financial, spiritual, and physical assistance into thousands of Haitian lives. The children enrolled in the school receive a meal—a soup stocked with the key nutrients they needed. This is often the only meal the children receive all day. Several of the kids brought bowls or containers that allowed them to take half their soup home to share with their families. One afternoon, I walked past two cute little boys. Trying to connect with them, I smiled and made a munching sound, "Mmm," as if the food was good. Without hesitation, the sweet little boy, already petite from dietary insufficiency, stuck his spoon out to offer me his soup. My heart crumbled. This little boy who literally was eating the only food he had, was so generously and, without reservation, was offering it to me.

Another girl from the orphanage whisked me away after one of our group events. She wanted to do my hair—a pastime many Haitian women enjoy. She showed me around the orphanage. There were bunks piled together in a large room. The girls' possessions were so minimal—what they owned was either in their bunk or a small locker. She proceeded to arrange my hair in cornrows. Wow, was that a painful experience on the scalp! This white girl could hardly handle it! While she was working on my hair (and I was attempting to hide my contorted, grimacing face), I complimented her on a black glittery bracelet she wore. I wanted her to feel pretty and desired to connect with her—woman to woman. Through the language barrier, I tried to ask about her dreams, hobbies, and family. She was only a teenager but had already faced such sadness. After my hair was done, she promptly ushered me to the mirror. She was so proud of her work. I praised her and thanked her for a job well done (although, I must confess—I'm too white to look good in cornrows—not a good look for me). As we stood next to the mirror, smiling and hugging each other, she reached to her wrist, pulled off her bracelet, and placed it on my wrist. My heart broke at this act of love extended to me. I tried to refuse it. I couldn't bear the idea that I would take one of this girl's only possessions when I had hundreds of jewelry pieces in an armoire at home. But she looked sad and offended at my refusal and insisted I take it. So I received it graciously and did all I could to show her my sincerest appreciation. Her gift was so humbling and so beautiful. The Haitians were showing me the purest side of generosity.

I could go on and on about the orange-haired children who were malnourished, the young man whose tent-like home flooded every time it rained, the precious girl we sponsored whose mother died of TB (unbeknownst to us) the day we chose to sponsor her, the incredible worship service, the children that swarmed us in the schoolyard, the little girl who wouldn't let go of me...the stories are endless. It's hard to summarize. The people we met were sincerely beautiful, inside and out. Their smiles are seared on our hearts. They carried in them a joy beyond the material world. They greeted us with gratitude and trust, never begging, never entitled. That trip reminded me that even on our worst day, we're profoundly blessed.

The point is not that wealth is bad or that our affluent country is sinful because of its prosperity. The point is that it's grievous to have much and to hoard with no concern for or generosity to those in need. The point is that it is wrong to think that we're entitled to all the overabundance of "stuff" with which we're blessed. The point is, it's against God's divine purpose for us to have much materially and spiritually and to give little to those in need. We were not called to live a life of wealth simply so we could live on cruise control. We were not called to be transformed by Christ just so that we're the nicer "Jones." We were given much and have been loved much so that we can love and give to others. What a shame— and I speak to myself here, as well—to waste a life, open, healthy, and able to serve God in radical, profound ways because of fear, greed, and entitlement. And sadly, I've habitually lost the point myself. I've stood on the brink of losing it all and have all too quickly found myself believing the lie that I actually deserve all I own and still have. This is the American trap. What we own is not really ours to begin with, and how we live is not merely for our own success. To die to self and live for God is both the challenge and the reward. To live for self and neglect your neighbor is both the root and nourishment of egocentrism.

Don't hate what you have, nor be resentful of your wealth. Don't despise your blessings of affluence or success. Don't belittle the fact that your paycheck is substantial or that your job has good benefits. Don't discredit the fact that you've worked hard and made educational, physical, and financial sacrifices to get to where you are today. These are accomplishments to be proud of. These are blessings—all very good indeed. These are opportunities to recognize that God does provide. We should not detest the overabundance we find ourselves blessed with in America, but what we should do is allow it to help us recognize that we can live with a lot less and give a lot more. We are so rich. I am so rich. Everything's a plus.

Chapter 17

A Thing or Two About Marriage

I began this book in my 736-square foot apartment nearly a decade ago. I was in a different phase of life then—starting my first real career-job, single, hopeful of the nearness of meeting my "soul mate," finishing graduate school, etc. This book developed on the cusp of old sorrows, the hopes of new beginnings, and the closures of daunting questions. After many edits, rereads, cut-outs, and markings, the old thoughts streaked the new realizations, coalescing into a description of my overall journey of belief. I find myself in a new space—a new place in life. Some of what I had yearned for a decade ago has come to fruition. I own a home. I'm married. I've moved on in life—finding victory in some areas and new challenges in others.

Almost five years ago, I met my now-husband, Chris. He caught me by surprise, at a time when I was finally very content with being single. And although, my deepest desire was to be married, I had reached a place where the urgency and desperation to date lay quietly in the corners of my heart, like an old toy waiting to be revisited at a more appropriate time. When I recount our story, I describe Chris as a "courtesy date." In other words, I didn't want to be rude by immediately saying "no" without really meeting him, so I thought, *one date, and it will be over.* But I liked him a little more than I expected...ok, maybe a lot more than I expected.

Chris and I were I guess what people would call "traditional" in how we did things. We dated for some time and didn't live together until we were married. Although I would say we knew each other intricately well before marriage, it's true that marriage and the commitment behind it bring you into a deeper realm of *everything*—a greater depth of emotional and physical intimacy, a fleshing out of spiritual connectedness, an unveiling of their habits, a holistic interpretation to their mental processing, and a more intense experience of disagreements. With the beauty of the depth comes the sacrifice and discomfort.

God has blessed me with a wonderful husband. He is a man who has sacrificed for me, for us, and our future. He has worked hard, abundantly providing more than we even need. He has stayed honorable and committed even when he has seen my ugliest and somehow still finds the ability to call me a "good woman" at the times I would disown myself, given the option. He is loving, motivated, passionate, tender, and can still make my heart skip a beat by the touch of his hand or with a glimpse of his smile. I'm head-over-heels in love with this man, and I soak up every ounce of attention he pours on me.

As with all areas of my fragile emotional tapestry, marriage has been fraught with its own set of explosive minefields. And although there are times in marriage when you feel like your heart's eye has caught a glimpse of the fullness and joy of Heaven, there are times when your core breaks to a point of what appears to be inconsolable disrepair. Your husband can set your heart on fire or burn it out. The power within a marriage was designed by God, meant to be strong, binding, and fierce. It remains in the control of the couple to wield this power into a helpful or hurtful force.

Like most people, I entered marriage with some known and

unknown expectations. Expectations are often beneficial, providing a standard to achieve a guidepost for direction and goals to attain. Like any double-edged sword, unmet expectations can result in discouragement or frustration. I have not been married long, but I've been married long enough to realize that some things exceed my expectations while other things don't even hit the target. Regardless, God has used marriage, and will continue to use it, as a way to reveal more about His character and my heart.

Often when a couple decides to marry they unite because they "love" their mate so much that they long to be with him or her above all others. It's a beautiful picture of how Christ chooses His bride, the Church—how He longs to unify Himself with the ones He loves, the children of God. Someone wants to spend the rest of their lives with that one special person who puts the air in their sails, the skip in their step, the cream in their coffee. There's a richness and closeness that they exclusively share, that is unique to them and is worth securing, declaring, and proclaiming in a legally binding agreement called marriage.

It's a beautiful thing, seeing the love of two people, the happiness in their unity and the respect they have for one another. I'm a stereotypical girl, and I love "love." I love weddings. I love chic flicks. I love romantic pursuits, first kisses, sweet notes, and sappy stories. Love is like the dessert in the buffet of life. And if I had my way, my diet would be indulgently filled with an excessive dose of this delightful delicacy. Going into marriage, however, with this gluttonous view of love may lead to damaging coronary effects.

The more we think that marriage is about us, the more we miss the powerful purpose God designed it for. "'For this reason a man will leave his father and mother and be united to his wife, and the two will become one flesh.' This is a profound mystery—but I'm talking about Christ and the church. However, each one of you also must love his wife as he loves himself, and the wife must respect her husband" (Ephesians 5:31–33). God's designs in life always point to a higher purpose—His unrelenting pursuit of the lost. The love of God is so vast, so nearly incomprehensible, that multiple analogies throughout Scripture are used in attempts to help His people understand this unfathomable love. He compares His guardianship as a shepherd to sheep. He likens his protection as a mother hen hiding the chicks under her wings. The relationship shared between God and Jesus is explained as one of a father and son. Jesus calls the disciples His brothers. One of the most powerful descriptions of Jesus' loving, passionate relationship to His followers (and my personal favorite) is Jesus as the bridegroom and the Church as His bride. It's a love above all loves—it's *agape* love—unconditional, sacrificial, redeeming, and fiercely committed, even to the point of death.

As a married woman, this is the type of love I strive for and yearn for from my man. We were designed to be unconditionally loved. It's what we long for and what we hope we find in our soul mate. We long for our spouse to see our worst and to love us unreservedly in the midst of it. We pray for unadulterated grace, edifying communication, selfless servitude, undefiled tenderness, merciful accountability, and absolute forgiveness. It's what we expect from our spouse. "Love is patient, love is kind. It does not envy, it does not boast, it is not proud. It does not dishonor others, it is not self-seeking, it is not easily angered, it keeps no record of wrongs. Love does not delight in evil but rejoices with the truth. It always protects, always trusts, always hopes, always perseveres. Love never fails" (1 Corinthians 13:4–8). This is what it's about. This is what we desire and strive to resemble, even ourselves.

The reality, however, doesn't seem to meet these expectations—the dream is deferred, the honeymoon is over, the roses and butterflies are dead. And although we may try and try, the daily result mirrors more the world than the undefiled love of Christ. Rome was not built in a day, and wars were not won in a battle. It is in the arduous back-and-forth of trench-treading where marriages are either made marvelous or mutilated.

The beauty of a Christ-centered marriage is that there are not only two fighting the good fight—there are three. It's the couple with the power of God working to accomplish His good and perfect will in and through the holy union. A Christian couple may face more opposition but have much less to fear. I believe that the Enemy has inflicted a full-fledged assault on the purity, sanctity, and importance of marriage because the Enemy is threatened by the powerful force behind a stable, secure, loving, and healthy relationship. If the Enemy can weaken a marriage, he can weaken multiple lives tied to that marriage. That is why it's essential to call on the help of God to protect, nourish, and heal your marriage.

Christian couples must recognize and acknowledge

that marriage is their primary ministry. It comes before church obligations, mission work, and dreams to do "big things" for God. Marriage is a God-given responsibility, and married couples are charged to maintain good stewardship of the task with which He has blessed you. In Colossians, Paul discusses his labor for the cause of Christ and the Church:

> Now I rejoice in what I am suffering for you, and I fill up in my flesh what is still lacking in regard to Christ's afflictions, for the sake of his body, which is the church. I have become its servant by the commission God gave me to present to you the word of God in its fullness— the mystery that has been kept hidden for ages and generations, but is now disclosed to the Lord's people. To them God has chosen to make known among the Gentiles the glorious riches of this mystery, which is Christ in you, the hope of glory. He is the one we proclaim, admonishing and teaching everyone with all wisdom, so that we may present everyone fully mature in Christ. To this end I strenuously contend with all the energy Christ so powerfully works in me (Col 1:24–29).

Paul participates in the suffering for the sake of the gospel— the glorious riches of the mystery of Christ within His people, the assurance of glory. This is his goal, his cause, so much so that he struggles to persevere with all the energy Christ so powerfully provides within him. Similarly, the life within marriage will often be seasoned with suffering and strenuous efforts. If marriage is a reflection of Christ and His Church, then should we not also anticipate sacrifice, hard work, and, at times, suffering?

I'm not saying that marriage should be full of blood, sweat, and tears, but I want to encourage the crying newlywed that this is part of the journey. God brings two (often very different) people with different upbringings, different perspectives, different annoying habits, food preferences, sleep schedules, etc., together in a small house and says, "Be fruitful and multiply" (Genesis 1:28). Naturally, some days will be fraught with opposition, and some days will be paved with pure joy. But the charge and challenge is to continue on—be fruitful in your ambitions, your speech, your service to one another, your sacrifice of your will for theirs, your loving submission to one another. Multiply in grace, affection, peace, patience, tenderness, and, of course...babies!

I've only just begun this journey—in no way can I offer the wisdom, experience, and depth of insight a married couple of ten, twenty, or fifty years can. But let me leave you with some thoughts that have been rolling around in my head.

Women, you have a God-given role to love, support, and submit to your husbands. I do not pretend to know what all that looks like. God as my witness, I have fallen flat on my face too many times in my best attempts, which quickly went south. However, what I know God has been impressing on my heart is to watch my tongue and defend my marriage. According to Ephesians 1:18–20,

> I pray that the eyes of your heart may be enlightened in order that you may know the hope to which he has called you, the riches of his glorious inheritance in his holy people, and his incomparably great power for us who believe. That power is the same as the

mighty strength he exerted when he raised Christ from the dead and seated him at his right hand in the heavenly realms.

There is deep richness in this passage to unpack. First, we must recognize that our hope and inheritance are in the Lord—not in our men. Time and time again, I've fallen because I turned to Chris instead of to God for approval, strength, and love. And although Chris should show love, attention, and affection, he isn't responsible for my self-worth. He can't grant my value, nor should I yield him the power to diminish my worth. Instead, we are reminded in Ephesians that God is the benevolent giver of His glorious inheritance. He's the one that bestows favor, spiritual strength, purpose, and unconditional love. His glorious inheritance is found in a love that has chosen to embrace even the ugliest of sinners. It is in this love that we find our worth, value, and security. Try as he might, no husband can ever grant that level of assurance or that rich of an inheritance.

Secondly, we must be aware of the God-given strength we possess. Women, we hold the power of God within us—the same mighty power that raised Christ from the dead is the power we can impart into our men and into our families. It's the power to grant us control over our tempers and tongues, the power that can heal the damage already tattering the seams of our households. Proverbs 18:21 reminds us that "The tongue has the power of life and death, and those who love it will eat its fruit." Every day, we hold the power of life and death in the words we speak into our marriage and about our men. We can tear down or build up our men and homes in a matter of a hot second by the words we choose. Jesus explains in Luke 6:45, "A good man brings good things out of the good stored up in his heart, and an evil man brings evil things out of the evil stored up in his heart. For the mouth speaks what the heart is full of." What we verbally spew ultimately stems from a heart issue. Yes, you are angry because of what he did, and yes, oftentimes, husbands can feel as though they were put on this earth simply to push every single button (even the ones you didn't know you had) but at the end of the day, what comes out of our mouths in response is a reflection of a deeper heart issue with God. This, though, is the beauty of marriage. It was not designed merely for mutual fulfillment but to draw us closer to God and, ultimately, to continue a sanctifying process so that our hearts eventually begin to mirror Jesus Christ more and more. Hopefully, most of us get fifty years to work on this sanctifying process, because Lord knows we need every second possible for true transformation. It's not for the faint of heart. But it's essential to remember that though our mouths may reek from an unkempt heart, God is using our men, our differences, the little annoyances and major blowouts to chip away the slime, dirt, and muck, all the while reminding us that we can withstand it because of the mighty power within us—the power that raised a dead man to life.

Ladies, although men are called to protect, we are called to defend our marriages. We need to be praying without ceasing for our men. It's our most powerful weapon, and the best way to understand the command in Ephesians 5:22: "Wives, submit yourselves to your own husbands as you do to the Lord." It isn't always easy to submit to these broken, macho, sometimes domineering, God-given counterparts we call husbands. They are fallen, and boy, do we know it. But again, just as our security and worth do not come from our men but from God, so likewise is our submission. We work and serve out of love for the Lord. Often we do it out of love for our husbands, but in those moments when you feel more "in-like" and less "in-love," we need to quickly remind ourselves that our Lord is God, and our responses are for Him (not "him"). It is hard, however, to keep this mindset when tempers are flying, feelings are battered, and rough patches feel like rough decades. This is when you pray. Ladies, pray like it's your job. Get on your knees, get in your corner, hunker down, and pray to the God who holds the mighty power that raised Jesus from the dead. Pray for your heart, pray for his heart, pray for change, pray for peace, pray for comfort, pray to be heard, pray to learn silence, pray to heal, pray for the "eyes of your heart to be enlightened." Pray, pray, pray. It's your mighty weapon, your sword, your shield, your defender of your marriage. If the Enemy is throwing every arrow possible, you are to take your shield of faith, your belt of truth, your helmet of salvation, and your sword of the Spirit, and pray for your marriage. "Pray without ceasing" (Thessalonians 5:17). Prayer not only helps protect your marriage, but it brings transformation in your own heart. "Therefore, confess your sins to each other and pray for each other so that you may be healed. The prayer of a righteous person is powerful and effective" (James 5:16). God will hear you and meet you in the desperation, the hurt, the joys, the sorrows, the rejoicing, and the victory.

Bitterness will continually try to creep in. It's so easy to get caught in the trap of what you wish you had instead of appreciating what you have. Throw in a dash of bitterness, and the searing torch of unforgiveness has officially branded your heart. The art of forgiveness is just that...an abstract, unpredictable, non-formulaic art. It is often complicated and layers deep, but press on to find full release and surrender. You can't change him, and he can't change you. You are in charge of you, and he is in charge of himself. You can't make him respond in the way you wish or repent as he should, but this is where you must again tap into the mighty power that raised Jesus from the cross. Forgiveness doesn't condone or justify. It does not even remove the emotion or hurt feelings, but it leads you toward your own heart to find freedom, peace, and release. For your own sake, seek forgiveness. Do not allow him or the situation to claim more territory that is rightfully yours.

Lastly, speak truth and blessing into your marriage. 1 Peter 3:10 says, "'Whoever would love life and see good days must keep their tongue from evil and their lips from deceitful speech.'" We've already touched on this some, but what we say holds power—for better or for worse. When you speak negatively about your husband or your situation, you begin to slide into a negative thought pattern. Quickly, your marriage can seem more unbearable and disappointing than the butterflies and rose-framed pictures you had in your mind when you said, "I do." What we say, we think. What we think, we act out. What we act out, we believe, and what we believe affects the core of who we are and our marriage. You must speak truth into your marriage, but what if the truth of your marriage is not positive and is ugly and dark? Then you must speak blessing and gratitude over your marriage. Speak about what you do have, what he does still do, what he refrains from doing, what parts of the week were pleasant, tolerable, good. Speak and focus on the blessing, and pray about the curse. Thank God for the plenty in spite of the scarcity. You must find the silver lining. You must bring that bit of truth, hope, and goodness to the One who can multiply it into abundance, just as He did with the fish and loaves for the five thousand. This, again, is not an easy task, but remember that marriage is not about "easy." It's loving like Christ—sacrificially in suffering—clinging to the glorious inheritance.

People are going to speak doubt, disapproval, and a whole slew of opinions into your marriage. It is your job to guard and sort what you allow in and what you keep out. Even well-meaning people will share concerns or angrily empathize with your hurt and pain. Although their empathy initially soothes your heart, it's easy for it to leave lasting marks of doubt or deep confirmation about disparaging thoughts toward your man. It's hard to know what to keep and what to throw out from the surrounding family and friends who support you on this bumpy road, but always know that God deems marriage to be very good. Any advice, thoughts, or empathic affirmation that begins to make you angrier toward your spouse, causes you to start questioning your commitment, or hardens the bitterness in your heart, must be cast out. This is not from God. It does not benefit you or your marriage. These are half-truths from trusted sources that Satan uses to gain leverage. Pray for blessing and strength to speak God's truth into the confusing consolation. Fight with truth against all attacks for the sake of your marriage.

Before we end, I would like to give a challenge to the guys. Ephesians 5:25–30 states,

Husbands, love your wives, just as Christ loved the church and gave himself up for her to make her holy, cleansing her by the washing with water through the word, and to present her to himself as a radiant church, without stain or wrinkle or any other blemish, but holy and blameless. In this same way, husbands ought to love their wives as their own bodies. He who loves his wife loves himself. After all, no one ever hated their own body, but they feed and care for their body, just as Christ does the church— for we are members of his body.

Men, this is no light task. You are to love your wife as Christ loved the Church. What did Christ do for the Church? He pursued her, He fought for her, He patiently worked with her to overcome sin, He prayed for her, He served her, He made His whole life about her, He did not give up on her, He worked tirelessly with her, He accepted her yet challenged her, He defended her, protected her, and, most importantly, died for her. Christ showed the ultimate sacrifice in giving up His own will, desires, comforts and life for the sake of her good, her redemption. Men, you are the Christ-like leader in your marriage. Live up to this calling. Press into the Lord to be filled with the strength to lovingly, patiently, and tenderly deal with your wives. Love them deeply, die to your right to be right, speak kindly, and embrace her not just physically but spiritually and emotionally, as well. She needs your God-given masculinity to bring out her God-given beauty. She looks for your leadership—servant leadership. Not the type that dominates her, forces your ways upon her, but in the way that serves her, empowers her, enriches her being and calls out her strengths. Pursue her like it is your first date, like she is the apple of your eye. And if you don't feel those affections any longer, pray to God to restore a love as strong as death and a passion as fierce as a blazing fire (Song of Solomon 8:6). She may have grown familiar or let herself go. She may have done things that aren't right. She may not be the sweetest apple in the pie, but she is yours, given to you by God to keep. Respect her differences. Partake in her laughter. Tell her you love her...often. Seek to hear her heart at all costs and never stop seeing the beauty nestled deep within her eyes. She is your treasure. Whether or not you treat her as such, you will one day answer to the God who entrusted her with you. Handle with care—treat with respect. Live righteously before God and before her. Your nobility will not go unnoticed.

To all Christian couples, seek God individually and together. Spiritual intimacy can be one of the deepest experiences shared. Get plugged into a church, find other couples in a similar phase of life as you, read the Bible together, and if nothing else, pray together every day. Live in laughter, have fun, and enjoy life with your mate. "The LORD God said, 'It is not good for the man to be alone. I will make a helper suitable for him'" (Genesis 2:18). Help each other always.

I have so much to learn, and I pray God grants me decades with my husband to figure it out or at least to make a few strides in the right direction. I do not pretend to know the answers to all the mysteries found in marriage. In fact, I find myself scratching my head in utter puzzlement more often than I find myself enjoying the benefits of victory, but I am convinced that God is 110% behind marriage, so He will do anything in His power to help us out despite the numerous failures. This chapter has not been written from a place of perfection, but instead, I wrote these words to remind myself of the truth I know deep inside on the days when I have marital amnesia and emotional Alzheimer's. And so, I continue on, and I pray, and I seek the Father of all things beautiful and pure that He might always protect, preserve, and perfect this beautiful, messy, sacred, rewarding thing called marriage.

Finally, all of you, be like-minded, be sympathetic, love one another, be compassionate and humble. Do not repay evil with evil or insult with insult. On the contrary, repay evil with blessing, because to this you were called so that you may inherit a blessing. For,

"Whoever would love life and see good days
must keep their tongue from evil
and their lips from deceitful speech.
They must turn from evil and do good;
they must seek peace and pursue it.
For the eyes of the Lord are on the righteous
and his ears are attentive to their prayer,
but the face of the Lord is against those who do evil."

Who is going to harm you if you are eager to do good? But even if you should suffer for what is right, you are blessed. "Do not fear their threats; do not be frightened." But in your hearts revere Christ as Lord. Always be prepared to give an answer to everyone who asks you to give the reason for the hope that you have.

(1 Peter 3:8–15)

Chapter 18

Manna for the Day

Langston Hughes, an African American jazz artist, wrote a poem called "Harlem," that goes as follows:

What happens to a dream deferred?

Does it dry up
like a raisin in the sun?
Or fester like a sore--
And then run?
Does it stink like rotten meat?
Or crust and sugar over--
like a syrupy sweet?

Maybe it just sags
like a heavy load.

Or does it explode?[25]

To each reader, this piece of art elicits a unique reply. This little poem has awakened from its slumber within the corners of my memory time and again this past decade. Intrigued by the concept of unfulfillment, this once high school literary reading assignment has echoed a subtle mantra felt during my twenties. Throughout relational challenges, struggles with prolonged singleness, a fire, death, health issues, job loss, financial strain, emotional volatility, and spiritual amnesia, the simple alliteration of a "dream deferred" with images of raisins seemed to have an aberrational presence with each unforeseen difficulty.

Many a dream has been deferred for me. But I have a

sneaking suspicion that I am not alone. Years of an ongoing "thwarted-plan" pattern, can admittedly make a person grow weary and burned out. But although struggle comes, you must still choose to feel. Although opposition is relentless, you must still choose to hope.

On the pinnacle of yet another major event coupled with another disappointment, I couldn't help but question, "I went through years of struggle for this?" Over the decade, I had pursued the charge, "Take delight in the LORD, and he will give you the desires of your heart" (Psalm 37:4). However, I found myself questioning the outcome. I questioned the promise—were these really the desires of my heart? But somehow, I knew it all came back to trust. I heard the unrelenting gentle whisper, "Do you trust Me?"

It's thematic throughout the Old and New Testaments that God allows believers to find themselves in impossible situations. It's as if it sets the stage for the final act, the act where God shows up and throws in a twist, a good ending. God makes a promise to Abraham that He will bless him with numerous decedents. But the promised child was delayed, and Abraham was confused as to whether he should keep waiting or take matters into his own hands, so he used his handmaid to conceive the supposed promised child. It was not until decades after the promise was fulfilled that the awaited child was born. He wasn't born to two young people. No, God raised the stakes and allowed two people past the age of childbearing to conceive. Why? To reveal His glory. Nothing is too great for this God. Or what about Joseph—you know, the "Amazing Technicolored

Dream Coat" guy? He received a dream from God in his youth that his brothers would one day bow to him and that he would be in a position of authority over them. But this fulfillment came decades after Joseph had been left to die in a water cistern, captured as a slave, and jailed for many years based on false accusations. After all the years and waiting, then comes the promise, the answer. Enough time had to pass for the bitterness and unforgiveness to be chiseled away. Or what about Jesus, the long-awaited Messiah? People didn't recognize Him because He wasn't coming in the form they expected. He didn't conquer Rome. He didn't kill the enemies. No, instead He was shamefully crucified, dead for three days; not until after He was raised to life does the promise make sense. Then they—some, not all—recognized the Messiah as the one who died to ransom a sin-captive world once and for all.

Trust is hard, because the promises tarry, and the endings come in packages we don't anticipate. We have creative wishes. We have plans on how things should go, and we know the way they "ought" to look. But when they don't, we find confusion. So many times God has reminded me over and over again that it's not about anticipating how I think it will all play out. It's not about the destination. It's about the step of faith for the moment. It's manna for the day.

When the Lord is leading the Israelites out of Egypt, He gives very specific instructions to Moses about the food arrangements. The people were complaining about not having enough food, and so God tells Moses that He is about to send food for the people. "I will rain down bread from heaven for you. The people are to go out each day and gather enough for that day. In this way I will test them and see whether they will follow my instructions" (Exodus 16:4). I find it interesting that God wants them to store only enough manna for the day, not for the week, not for the month...for the day. And then the passage goes on to say that, basically, God is using this instruction to build their faith. Do they trust Him? If they trust Him, they will not hoard, but if they don't trust Him to provide food or enough of it, then the people will show their doubt by attempting to store up more manna. The people were in the desert, already hungry and tired from traveling—they had what we would consider to be a reasonable amount of discomfort to warrant their complaints and doubts about this "sovereign plan of God." They must have been thinking, "Were we released as slaves from Egypt only to be starving, tired, and hungry in the desert land? Where's the Promised Land? This is all the better it gets?" I get it. I'd be the grumbling Israelite that says, "Really, Lord? This is the best you can do?" But it's that attitude that kept them in the desert for forty years on what historians and Bible scholars unanimously agree should have taken only eleven days. The people weren't ready for the promise. They could not see or trust that they would receive their daily portion of manna and attribute the provision to God's faithfulness. How much more would they fail to rest in God's faithfulness in the Promised Land?

It's manna for the day, mercy for the moment, provision for the present. Jesus Himself says in Matthew 6:34, "Therefore do not worry about tomorrow, for tomorrow will worry about itself. Each day has enough trouble of its own." Even Jesus reminds us that there is enough in one day to deal with and says it's not for us to already (in advance) be fretting about the unknown future. Every time people asked Jesus specifics about the timing of when He would return for His Second Coming, He would simply remind them that it's not something to be concerned about. We have today to focus on...we need not overwhelm ourselves with the possible problems of tomorrow, next week, next year...today is full enough. The book of Lamentations is exactly that... a very sorrowful, melancholy book. Nearly every verse is dark, but within the five chapters of this book of misery, there is one small tiny flicker of light. In chapter 3, verses 23–26, the author pens,

> Because of the Lord's great love we are not consumed, for his compassions never fail. They are new every morning; great is your faithfulness. I say to myself, "The Lord is my portion; therefore I will wait for him." The Lord is good to those whose hope is in him, to the one who seeks him; it is good to wait quietly for the salvation of the Lord.

There it is again...we are not consumed by the perplexities, the adversity, and hardships of this life...why? Because His mercies are new every morning. Manna for the day. The grace imparted to us today will be enough for this day. I can't hoard it, I can't worry about it, I can't cling to what I think will get me through to next week and next year, and what if I get hurt, or what if someone dies, and what if the money runs out, or what if...no—He provides for us enough for the moment at hand. Though it may seem scarce, though it may be manna and not the four-course meal of steak and potatoes, it is sustenance that He knows we need. He knows that it's enough to carry us through until His next provision.

Should the manna run out, a new portion will be given. Trust is not about knowing the ending, it's about knowing the One who holds the ending. It's not over yet—He is still working. One step of faith leads to another step of faith, which leads to another step of faith. When we arrive at the ending, we appreciate its unique reassembled beauty. No, it's not what we expected. Is it better, perhaps? I don't know...it depends, I suppose. What you do with a dream deferred? Do you let it dry up like a raisin shriveled by the scorching sun? Do you let the unfulfillment, the trials, and the pain suck up all the sweet splendor from the plump grape it once was? Or do you let the dream deferred fester—does the heartache drill into your being to the point the pain makes you close fast the shutters on the window of your soul? Do you let a dream deferred rot so that the bitterness permeates all who come in contact with you? Or perhaps it's a burden—a load that weighs down even the brightest of days. But maybe, just maybe, you allowed this deferred dream to crust over like a sweet apple pie—baked by the heated challenges and crystalized like a syrup—a melted mix of richness. I suppose that maybe a dream deferred could do much more in the hand of God than in the hand of man. Yes indeed, maybe the One who holds the dream says, "Let me *let it* explode to something more, something you could not conjure up." "Now to him who is able to do immeasurably more than all we ask or imagine, according to his power that is at work within us, to him be glory in the church and in Christ Jesus throughout all generations, for ever and ever! Amen" (Ephesians 3:20–21).

You see, each day we hold an ounce of trust and an ounce of perspective in our hand. An ounce for the day—not an ounce for the week, not an ounce for the year, not an ounce to carry us to the end... no, a proper portion for the day. Yes, He is still working. Cling tightly to the provision for the day, because when He leads you home, when the question is answered and the mystery is solved, you will be ready for the explosion of glory at hand.

Chapter 19

Everybody has their reasons. "No, I don't like lasagna because it gives me heartburn." "This diet is the best way to lose weight." "The Paleo diet is better." "I will never vote Democrat." "I will never vote Republican." Opinions, beliefs, convictions, and just plan ole' preferences are a dime a dozen. And I've added another dime to that dozen. The varying views and the heated debates add flavor to our society, to our lives. It's good to have competing perspectives, alternate points of view. It's necessary—sort of a checks and balances, if you will. We sharpen one another, challenge one another, ignite passion, and hearten change.

I think that a part of the reason some people are apprehensive in becoming a Christian is because they fear that they will lose this ability to spar and speak their mind. Many believe that they will lose their identity, in a sense. Perhaps they fear they will be bored or take on the appearance of radical fanatics who care only about Jesus and nothing else. Christianity seems to offer them a narrowed view of life and threatens to strip away autonomy. Many fear that Christianity will put the kibosh on individuality and that they'll miss out on the fun. Some have intellectual reservations. They feel forced to choose between science and the Bible. The authenticity of the ancient book seems outdated or inaccurate.

I've been through this, I understand. When you feel that your intellect, your aspirations, and your beliefs are bigger than a religious system, God becomes awfully small, and the idea of pursuing this invisible Being feels uncomfortably confining. I spent nearly two solid years shelving Christianity, educating myself on other religions, and trying to understand what I believed and why. What I can assure you is that truth rises to the top. What I found literally changed my life. God met me in the question. When I was trying to push Him away, He still managed to answer each question and doubt I presented. If you seek, if you question, if you doubt, keep pressing on to the end. Finish the inquiry, tackle it head-on. Pursue an ending, a sense of closure on the matters that instigated the quest.

During those two years, I felt very lost, but I discovered a lot about religion, science, and the gods of other cultures. I learned about the reliability of the original manuscripts of Scripture and the reliability of other archeological findings. I was surprised to hear that the authenticity is pretty lock-tight. I uncovered the similarities and differences of other religions and the contradictions within each. I found that I didn't have to choose between science and God but rather that God was the Author of science. The truth I found in science was the truth established by God. I exposed false interpretations of the Bible by revealing proof texting of biblical passages, verses, and even entire books.

There is so much I learned during that time, but one of the greatest gifts I gleaned was the awareness that God is so much bigger than I credited Him to be. That realization continues even now. The more I learn about God, the more my brain is stretched. In our homes and churches, we have these pretty portraits of Jesus with long hair and a docile face, but when we read Scripture and they try to describe God, the authors can't even fully capture His magnificence. They use analogies, colors, and symbols just to try and give some semblance to what they know. "I saw the glory of the God of Israel coming from the east. His voice was like the roar of rushing waters, and the land was radiant with his glory" (Ezekiel 43:2). Revelation 4:2–6:

> At once I was in the Spirit, and behold, a throne stood in heaven, with one seated on the throne. And he who sat there had the appearance of jasper and carnelian, and around the throne was a rainbow that had the appearance of an emerald. Around the throne were twenty-four thrones, and seated on the thrones were twenty-four elders, clothed in white garments, with golden crowns on their heads. From the throne came flashes of lightning, and rumblings and peals of thunder, and before the throne were burning seven torches of fire, which are the seven spirits of God, and before the throne there was as it were a sea of glass, like crystal.

We have an indescribable God—someone whose grandeur cannot be measured. And this is very good, good news.

Although churches may try to limit you, religion tries to stifle you, and God's people hypocritically and habitually fail you, the Author of it all transcends the system. The Creator invites creation to partake in the cosmic unfolding. A life pursing the living God is far from boring. He's always beckoning you deeper, higher, and calling you to go to unattainable places so that His abilities to make possible the impossible are revealed. If God is the Creator, then it only makes sense that He enjoys creating, developing, expressing—humans were born out of this abundance. We were created not out of scarcity to meet a need or longing within the Trinity; we were rather created out of the fullness of love to know and to be known.

Many of us walk around with apathetic lives. We numb the mundanity with busyness, careers, friends, being head of the PTA, or catching up on our Netflix shows. Is this really all there is? We go to school, we graduate, we get married, we have kids, we get divorced, we join a gym, we shovel snow, we cook dinner, and we retire at age 67. Is this what it's all about—our lives summed up in one run-on sentence? It seems lacking, doesn't it? We attain the dream job, the dream car, the dream spouse, and then what? We find ourselves in a nursing home and forgetting what we ate for breakfast? We get consumed with our social media—how many likes, what's new on Instagram, does my kitchen look like the one on Pinterest...on and on. We search for life and create life in our media-centric domains and fail to connect to the richer life God offers. It's like we've filled up on a fast food sandwich and missed the nutritious gourmet spread.

Many cultures lack fresh water or have the deadly oppression of rampant disease, but we don't have that in America. Instead, we have the silent killer known as apathy. We strive for the cookie-cutter house with the white picket fence and let out a sigh of acceptance when we secure half of that. I'm not proposing a health and wealth gospel, here. It's quite the opposite. Following God comes with a cost—it demands something of you. It makes you sacrifice and die to self—daily. And that's just it, that's what makes it worth it. To sum it up in the words of Martin Luther King, Jr., "If you've got nothing worth dying for, you've got nothing worth living for."[26]

Every good thing comes with a cost. Anything worthwhile takes effort but pays dividends. Following God is an adventure—there is never a dull moment. He's always calling us to do more. And steps of faith are strangely multiplied in His hands. I've already mentioned the story in the gospel in which Jesus is with a large crowd, five thousand people, who all need to be fed. All they had were five loaves of bread and two fish. But Jesus gave thanks and broke the bread, so that it would feed and satisfy the thousands. God is in the business of making much out of little. When we give Jesus even just a small step of trust, it can have exponential effects. Just as the bread was broken so that it could be multiplied, so it is with our lives in order for the abundance and worth of our existence can be multiplied. I would argue that although some have lost their identity in religion, an authentic relationship with Jesus can reunite them with their true identity—the one originally bestowed. Jesus brings life from death. He seems to really enjoy this task and as you follow Him, you continually see resurrection and restoration of the things that were once broken.

Luke 19:11–27 is a parable told by Jesus to show that with faith comes risk and with risk comes reward:

> As they heard these things, he proceeded to tell a parable, because he was near to Jerusalem, and because they supposed that the kingdom of God was to appear immediately. He said therefore, "A nobleman went into a far country to receive for himself a kingdom and then return. Calling ten of his servants, he gave them

ten minas, and said to them, 'Engage in business until I come.' But his citizens hated him and sent a delegation after him, saying, 'We do not want this man to reign over us.' When he returned, having received the kingdom, he ordered these servants to whom he had given the money to be called to him, that he might know what they had gained by doing business. The first came before him, saying, 'Lord, your mina has made ten minas more.' And he said to him, 'Well done, good servant! Because you have been faithful in a very little, you shall have authority over ten cities.' And the second came, saying, 'Lord, your mina has made five minas.' And he said to him, 'And you are to be over five cities.' Then another came, saying, 'Lord, here is your mina, which I kept laid away in a handkerchief; for I was afraid of you, because you are a severe man. You take what you did not deposit, and reap what you did not sow.' He said to him, 'I will condemn you with your own words, you wicked servant! You knew that I was a severe man, taking what I did not deposit and reaping what I did not sow? Why then did you not put my money in the bank, and at my coming I might have collected it with interest?' And he said to those who stood by, 'Take the mina from him, and give it to the one who has the ten minas.' And they said to him, 'Lord, he has ten minas!' 'I tell you that to everyone who has, more will be given, but from the one who has not, even what he has will be taken away. But as for these enemies of mine, who did not want me to reign over them, bring them here and slaughter them before me.'"

When we see Christianity as untrue, when we doubt the nature of God and view Him as a harsh taskmaster, we withhold. And when we withhold, we settle for predictability, entertainment, and filling our lives with numbing fluff.

To each of us, God has given a purpose. For some, it is found in their career. For others, it's found outside of their career. Sometimes it's found in the simple task of washing dishes. The point is, when you do it all to the glory of God (Colossians 3:23), the menial tasks become Kingdom advances.

There's a lot of life to live. In your short time on this planet, you've been called to contribute your autonomy. Don't waste your time. Don't waste your potential. Don't slide into the comfortable attire of apathy. You were made for greatness. God has written on your heart dreams and passions. Chase them—run with every ounce of energy you have. You've been crowned with glory and honor (Psalm 8:6), so press into this reality. Pioneer the unknown land. You were made to explore, to conquer, and to navigate uncharted territory. Dig deep, think big, submerge yourself in the splendor of your surroundings. Today is the day to live. You do not have the promise of tomorrow, so exhaust the riches of the present. Hold on to inspiration and grant yourself permission to be happy. You have a race to run, a purpose to fulfill, a hope to secure. It's not that people don't dream—it's that they don't dream big enough...DREAM!

> Therefore, since we are surrounded by such a great cloud of witnesses, let us throw off everything that hinders and the sin that so easily entangles. And let us run with perseverance the race marked out for us, fixing our eyes on Jesus, the pioneer and perfecter of faith. (Hebrews 12:1–2)

References

1.) Christians, Ian. *Discovering Classical Music*. Barnsley, South Yorkshire: Pen & Sword Books Ltd., 1988. 2016. Accessed October 15, 2017. https://books.google.com/books?id=wIptDQAAQBAJ&pg=PT217&lpg=PT217&dq=You will begin to write a concerto%E2%80%A6You will work with great facility%E2%80%A6The concerto will be of excellent quality&source=bl&ots=R8i6OTPm_R&sig=FQjob-gR5lOQCXndT1yzf4pRKLXs&hl=en&sa=X&ved=0ahUKEwjjnJCIgPTWAhVj2IMKHcbTDVcQ6AEILT-AB#v=onepage&q=You%20will%20begin%20to%20write%20a%20concerto%E2%80%A6You%20will%20work%20with%20great%20facility%E2%80%A6The%20concerto%20will%20be%20of%20excellent%20quality&f=false

2.) Kuntz, Danielle. "Out from the Depths of Hell: The Reception of Rachmaninoff." Music 242: Spring 2014. May 13, 2014. Accessed October 15, 2017. https://pages.stolaf.edu/music242-spring2014/portfolio/out-from-the-depths-of-hell-the-reception-of-rachmaninoff/

3.) *Eat Pray Love*. Directed by Ryan Murphy and produced by Dede Gardner. Performed by Julia Roberts, Julia Havier Bardem, James Franco, Richard Jenkins. USA: Sony, 2010. Film.

4.) Bell, Rob . Grand Rapids, MI: Zondervan, 2007.

5.) 2011 FAMILY DINNERS REPORT FINDS TEENS WHO HAVE INFREQUENT FAMILY DINNERS LIKELIER TO SMOKE, DRINK, USE MARIJUANA. The National Center on Addiction and Substance Abuse. September 22, 2011. Accessed October 17, 2017. https://www.centeronaddiction.org/newsroom/press-releases/2011-family-dinners-report-finds-teens-who-have-infrequent-family-dinners

6.)   Mounce, William D., D. Matthew Smith, and Miles V. Van Pelt, eds. *Mounce's Complete Expository Dictionary of Old & New Testament Words*. Grand Rapids, MI: Zondervan, 2006, 461–462.

7.)   McPherson, Casey. "New Morning." Recorded April 25, 2010. In *New Morning*. Alpha Rev. David Kahne, 2010, MP3.

8.)   Mounce, William D., D. Matthew Smith, and Miles V. Van Pelt, eds. *Mounce's Complete Expository Dictionary of Old & New Testament Words*. Grand Rapids, MI: Zondervan, 2006, 518–519.

9.)   Strong, James. *The New Strong's Exhaustive Concordance of the Bible*. Nashville, TN: Thomas Nelson Publishers, 2010, 334.

10.)   Horton, Michael. *The Christian Faith; A Systematic Theology for Pilgrims on the Way*. Grand Rapids, MI: Zondervan, 2011, Chapter 6 Section 4 Navigating Between Scylla and Charybdis.

11.)   Mounce, William D., D. Matthew Smith, and Miles V. Van Pelt, eds. *Mounce's Complete Expository Dictionary of Old & New Testament Words*. Grand Rapids, MI: Zondervan, 2006, 303.

12.)   Horton, Michael. *The Christian Faith; A Systematic Theology for Pilgrims on the Way*. Grand Rapids, MI: Zondervan, 2011, Chapter 6 Section 1 Defining Impassibility.

13.)   Horton, Michael. *The Christian Faith; A Systematic Theology for Pilgrims on the Way*. Grand Rapids, MI: Zondervan, 2011, Chapter 6 Section 2 Evaluating the Doctrine of Impassibility.

14.)   Horton, Michael. *The Christian Faith; A Systematic Theology for Pilgrims on the Way*. Grand Rapids, MI: Zondervan, 2011, 248-249.

15.)   Horton, Michael. *The Christian Faith; A Systematic Theology for Pilgrims on the Way*. Grand Rapids, MI: Zondervan,

2011, 249.

16.) Horton, Michael. *The Christian Faith; A Systematic Theology for Pilgrims on the Way.* Grand Rapids, MI: Zondervan, 2011, 253.

17.) Kilgore, Donald. "Gungor 'Ghosts Upon the Earth' Official EPK". August 2011. YouTube video, 4:39. August 2011. https://www.youtube.com/watch?v=zGtvtLDicwA

18.) Gungor, Michael. "This Is Not The End." In *Ghosts Upon the Earth*. Gungor. Brash Records, 2011, CD.

19.) Lewis, C.S. *A Grief Observed.* HarperCollins Publishers, 2001, 27-28

20.) Groves, Sara. "What I Thought I Wanted." Recorded January 11, 2005. In *The Other Side of Something*. Sara Groves. 2004 Sponge Records, 2005, CD.

21.) Collins, Francis . *The Language of God.* New York: Free Press, 2006.

and

The American Heritage Dictionary of the English Language. 2017. Accessed October 17, 2017. https://ahdictionary.com/word/search.html?q=miracle.

22.) Matthews, Dave. "Gray Street." Recorded July 16, 2002. In *Busted Stuff*. Dave Matthews Band. RCA Records Label, 2002, CD.

23.) Mike Bickle, Song of Solomon sermon series.

24.) Yohannan, K. P. Revolution in World Missions. Carrollton, TX: gfa books, a division of Gospel for Asia, 2004.

25.) Hughes, Langston. "Harlem." Poetry Foundation. Accessed October 18, 2017. https://www.poetryfoundation.org/poems/46548/harlem.

26.) "Martin Luther King, Jr." AZ Quotes. Accessed October 18, 2017. http://www.azquotes.com/quote/1123036.

All references used were for the enrichment of this book. The authors and reference sources in their entirety do not represent the religious, political, or personal affiliation of Rebecca Greenfield unless otherwise stated in this book

Not Sure About Jesus?

Doubting my faith and seeking the truth proved to be the most life-changing, healthy risk in my life. If you are not sure about Jesus, please don't give up. Take your questions, fears, and apprehensions and seek answers. My only request is that once you start, don't stop until you have reached a logical conclusion. I cannot claim to remember all the endless books, articles, videos, or academic research that I used to find the answers to all my doubts on Christianity, but on the next page are a few resources that did help me significantly throughout the quest. I hope you find them helpful as well. Should you run into some bumps along the way, please reach out via my website:

www.Rebecca-Greenfield.com

Recommended Sources

Blue Like Jazz by Donald Miller

Everything is Spiritual by Rob Bell—(video)

Mere Christianity by C.S. Lewis

Richard Dawkins and John Lennox Debates—(video)

Searching for God Knows What by Donald Miller

The Case for Christ by Lee Strobel

The Cross of Christ by John Stott

The Language of God by Francis Collins

Various academic books on other world religions—(easily found at a college library)

Velvet Elvis by Rob Bell

Why the Jews Rejected Jesus by David Klinghoffer

Please note, source recommendations in their entirety do not represent my religious affiliation or specific viewpoints.

Start Your Journey with Jesus

Maybe you've decided to take a chance on Jesus, but you're not sure where to get started. Living for Christ is kind of like a marriage. There's a point where you finally decide, "Hey, this is a commitment I want to make for my life," and then you spend the rest of the time, walking it out with the One you committed your life to. You travel the highs and lows, but you claim that One as your own and that One claims you. So, if you are ready to make a point of commitment, simply tell God something like this:

Hi God. I want to know you more. I am ready to learn what it means to follow You, love You and be loved by You. Please forgive me for my sins, the things that have kept me away from You. I want to turn away from these things and start living a life for You instead. Thank You for forgiving me and chasing after me. I believe and trust that because Your son, Jesus, died on the cross for my sins, I can now seek and find forgiveness. I thank You that You no longer have wrath towards me, but complete love, mercy and grace. May You please become the Lord of my life, my heart, my mind and my soul. I invite the Holy Spirit to work in my heart so that I can draw close to You. Thank you for all You do. In the power and authority of Jesus Christ, Amen

If you've decided to make Christ a bigger part of your life, and you want to let me know, please feel free to email me at contact@ rebecca-greenfield.com. I'd love to hear from you! I encourage you to get involved with other people who also make Jesus a big part of their lives. Go to church, join a group, start praying... do something! If nothing else, start reading your Bible and at least visit a local church community. Sometimes it takes awhile to find the right place, but when you do, it's so worth it.

May you feel the smile of God beaming down on you as you start your new journey—welcome home!

Acknowledgements

Thank you for the quiet work crew who labored tirelessly behind the scenes. I am so thankful for you all!

Blurb Writers—Thank you Pastor Cody Clark, Pastor Robin Hart, Jenny Kuhns, and Pastor Jeff Martell for taking time out of the busy holiday season to read my book and provide feedback. I am so appreciative for the sacrifice of time you made to help me out. Thank you for the tremendous support, encouragement, and kindness you have shown.

Erin Gill—Thank you for your friendship for so many years and continued support throughout the seasons of life. Your photographic eye and uncanny way of being real with me was exactly what I needed. Thank you for the professional photos, the yummy ice cream in thirty-degree weather, always knowing how to speak truth into my life and your sincere love.

Jennie Gold—Thank you for your eagerness to work on book design. Your knowledge with typesetting, cover creation and digital conversion is beyond my skillset and something I have loved partnering with you on. You are so gifted. Between your heart and your talents, I know God will use you in big ways. Thank you for your creativity, openness and willingness to tackle any idea I conjured up. I couldn't have done it without you.

Sarah Klish—I am still so thankful, God put us in the same kindergarten class so that we could be friends for life. You have been such a special and dear friend to me throughout the years and I am so grateful that even into our thirties we are still so close. Thank you for your excitement and willingness to work on T-shirt design despite being a busy mother of three. Thank you also, to your wonderful husband, Joe, for the part I know he played behind the scenes. Your creativity, artistic abilities and generous hearts individually and as a couple have been more helpful than you know. Kindergarten Kids Forever!

Sarah Najimian—Thank you, not only for your close friendship over the many years, but your willingness to help me at the drop of a hat. Thank you for answering the plethora of questions, always picking up your phone every time I called, and the late night, creative, last-minute tweaks. You never complained once but worked creatively and innovatively to produce a website I absolutely love. You've poured countless hours into helping me and I am humbled by all the ways you've continued to support me. I am so thankful for our years of history, our four-hour long evening talks, the laughter shared over my technological ineptitude and the God-honoring, trusted friend that you are and always have been. I love being creative with you!

Run the Race Marked Out Before You

Arms Back, Heart Abandoned.

Hebrews 12:1-2

Visit my website at

www.Rebecca-Greenfield.com

CPSIA information can be obtained
at www.ICGtesting.com
Printed in the USA
FFOW02n0043080118
44305520-43919FF

9 780692 988008